The Snipers
We Couldn't See

A MEMOIR

OF GROWING UP

WITH MY MOTHER'S

SCHIZOPHRENIA

The Snipers We Couldn't See

A MEMOIR

OF GROWING UP

WITH MY MOTHER'S

SCHIZOPHRENIA

KAREN COMBA

— BEAVER'S POND PRESS —

SAINT PAUL, MINNESOTA

Edited by Kerry Stapley
Book design and typesetting by Athena Currier
Managing Editor: Hanna Kjeldbjerg

ISBN 13: 978-1-64343-818-4
Library of Congress Catalog Number: 2021918475
Printed in the United States of America
First Edition: 2022
26 25 24 23 22   5 4 3 2 1

Beaver's Pond Press
939 West Seventh Street
Saint Paul, MN 55102
(952) 829-8818
www.BeaversPondPress.com

To order, visit www.KarenComba.com.

Contact the author at www.KarenComba.com for speaking engagements, book club discussions, and interviews.

This book is dedicated to the mother I wish I had gotten the chance to get to know.

Friends of my mother tell me how incredible, fun, and giving she was to anyone in need. She loved her family and fell head over heels in love with my father. I still find myself sad that mental illness robbed my siblings and me of the joy of having our mom well.

Mom, I will not let your life go down in vain. In your honor, I promise to fight for families like ours.

MOM, DON'T GO

T he morning my mother took her life was a cold, cloudy, dreary January day. Apart from the particularly glum weather, the day began like any other. I awoke before my husband and children. I looked out the kitchen window and watched the cold water running fast in the river behind our home. The huge cottonwood tree leaning over the riverbank was bare, having lost its leaves months earlier. It was easy, that morning, to see the pair of bald eagles perched at the top beside their nest. I reached for the coffeepot to start morning breakfast. I thought about what to fix. Given the cold, damp weather, I settled on Cream of Wheat cereal and scrambled eggs. I moved to the hallway. My children's bedroom doors were open, and I could see both kids at once, sleeping soundly. I cherished this quiet second before the craziness of the day began.

"Kids, time to rise and shine!" I waited long enough to see two pairs of eyes open. Then I turned and went back to the kitchen. I got out four glasses for orange juice, two mugs for coffee, and the creamer. "Breakfast is ready!" Like clockwork, we were all sitting down and starting the day. They spoke of their plans—sports practices, and what was going on at school: which assignments were coming due, and when they had upcoming tests. I sipped my coffee and let my mind drift.

As a dental assistant and manager in my husband's practice, I was supposed to be at work by eight o'clock. And yet, the sensation of my mom's "presence" was unusually strong. My husband felt my uneasiness. His arms were around me when a chill ran through me. I told him I was worried about her, and he urged me to go see my mother.

While I was driving the short distance to my parents' home, I thought about my own life and how it had been affected by growing up with a mentally ill mother. My mom had been in and out of mental hospitals since I was five years old. Shock treatments, multiple medications, and countless, long hospital stays had all dramatically altered her perspective toward family and life in general. Growing up, I never knew when the slightest provocation might send her into a tirade of anger, resulting in horrible, hurtful words, or worse—a severe beating.

I slipped back to the present as I pulled into the yard of my parents' home. My mom was startled when I walked into the house.

"What are you doing here?" she asked.

"I just felt I had to come," I replied.

My dad walked in smiling from the daily farm chores. "Hey, have you been fired?" he joked.

We visited for a while, and then a nostalgic mood hit us. We went downstairs to the old trunk and dug out the family photos. Warm memories of the past enveloped us all. For two joyful hours, we laughed. Once again, I heard all about our family history, except this time, I listened. Finally, my dad had to leave to take some machinery parts into town for repairs.

The fun of the morning clouded over when a wave of mental anguish hit Mom. She said she didn't feel well.

"I want to kill myself," she told me in a clear, determined voice.

Terror settled in the room. My heart was ice, and my eyes saw only a gray haze. I could not see her face, and her voice suddenly sounded far away and muffled. As I struggled to listen, Mom's dread of another mental breakdown and its devastating effect on her family was pushing her to the limit.

"Do you know what it's like to have 350,000 ants crawling out of your skin?" Her voice mirrored her pain.

I felt uncertain how to help.

"Shall I call a doctor? Maybe get your medicine?" I asked, grasping for straws. She stood in a daze with a blank, frozen stare and said nothing. Time stopped while we waited for Dad to return. I pulled him aside and told him what she'd said. A gray, haggard look came over him, his face reflecting his worry. I told Dad I would go to the dental office and finish out the afternoon, then return that evening and stay for a few days.

I was in the doorway, ready to leave, when my mother suddenly grabbed my face in both her hands and kissed me. "I will miss you more than anything. I love you. Take care of your dad."

My mind went numb. It sounded as though she was saying good-bye, but I didn't want to acknowledge that. She'd said crazy things many times before. I hoped this was just another one of her episodes that would end with a brief return of sanity. I hoped this to be true, even though a nagging feeling in my gut told me this time might be different.

"I love you, too," I weakly answered. "And I'll be back shortly." I glanced at the clock on the wall and was surprised to see it was only twelve o'clock.

At the dental office, I told my husband about my morning with my parents and my feelings of apprehension. Aware of my mother's mental problems, he agreed with my decision to stay with them for a few days, and we decided I should go immediately after work. The afternoon dragged, and I found it increasingly difficult to keep my mind focused on routine duties. The final patient of the day was being dismissed when the phone rang.

"Are you alone?" asked the voice. I barely recognized that it belonged to my dad.

"No," I replied.

His voice shook, but it got louder and firmer as he asked the question again. "*Are you alone?*"

My heart was in my throat. "No, what is it?"

His voice changed to a scream, like none I had ever heard. "Your mom did it." I knew right in that moment what he meant. Mom had taken her own life. She'd carried out her threat.

"She's still warm. Help me . . . who . . . what . . . do I need to do?"

But I couldn't help him. I couldn't do anything. I felt life drain out of me as I hurled the phone against the wall, breaking it. An agonized, primal outcry of pain and protest let loose. I was losing time . . . losing my mind . . . losing my strength, I pictured myself in my dad's arms saying, "Why didn't I stay?"

The guilt of leaving my mother shrouded me in cold darkness. I was twenty-nine years old, a motherless child, lost in the repercussions of mental illness. It was an ugly day for my soul. Her kiss before I left came racing back into my head. The words *Take care of your dad* echoed in my mind. She was telling me she was going to leave us. My mind screamed at me. *You should have known what she meant! It's all your fault! You're so stupid.*

Why did I ever leave her? If I had stayed, could I have saved her? If I'd stayed, maybe she'd still be alive. Maybe she wouldn't have taken a whole bottle of sleeping pills. And yet, amid the guilt there was another emotion—one I had never before felt for my mother—unconditional love. I only recognized it because in that exact moment, that love had been ripped from my life. Mom left a note taped to the door so Dad would see it before he came into the house:

> *Most people will call this suicide, but it really is an Act of Love. I'm scared I will get so confused, I will not remember my own family. They don't know how to help me yet, and I am fearful of ending up in a nursing home, looking out the window, unable to know anything that is going on around me. I'm afraid they will take our farm. Richard, you have worked too hard to have to lose everything in order to take care of me. I will see you again, and next time, I will be well.*
>
> *Love, Evelyn.*

Later that day, we learned that she had gone to see her brother at lunch. He told us that she came into the café, walked up to him at the table, put her arms around him, hugged him, and said, "You know I love you." Then she turned and left. Because of all her past erratic behavior, he didn't make anything of it.

THE BEGINNING

M y grandmother would often talk to me about the love my parents shared. When Grandmother talked about their love, she inevitably remembered her own husband. Tears would well up in her eyes as she reminisced about her marriage. "This kind of love doesn't come along every day," she would say. "Just like I was fortunate, so was your mother, with the kind of love your father has been able to give her."

My dad was born into a loyal, honest, hardworking farm family. He learned the value of a full day's work and never shied away from responsibility. He met my mother in high school, and they fell madly in love. My grandmother kept numerous pictures scattered all over the top of her dresser. Each one was in its own little frame, set atop a handmade doily. One of the pictures stood out to me. It was of my mom and dad. Mom's face was slightly turned, and her smile was so big, it showed all her teeth. The plaid flannel shirt sleeve of my dad's arm was around her tiny frame. I noticed her hair: curly waves without a strand out of place. My dad's eyes looked so shiny behind his stylish round gold wire-rim glasses. Mom's dark-red lipstick seemed to show

how perfectly shaped her lips were. Mom and Dad seemed like they were having the best date night ever. They both had such flirtatious looks on their faces.

Mom graduated at the age of sixteen. She went to the University of Lincoln to become a teacher. Dad was two years younger than Mom. He finished high school and worked on his folks' farm. He and Mom continued their courting. Mom graduated from college and started teaching kindergarten through eighth grade in a one-room country school. It was near her folks' farm, so she lived at home. Dad enlisted in the army and became an MP. They were engaged before he left for Korea, where he would be stationed from September 1953 to the fall of 1955. Mom continued teaching, saving every cent so they could buy a farm when he returned.

My grandmother Ella spoke highly of my mother's passion for education. According to Ella, Mom would teach all day, then stay after school to help any child who did not have an A or B average. My mother believed no child should leave her classroom without at least a C average. She always said, "If the child is at a C or D level, it just means our brains are not connecting, so we will work together until our wires connect and they get it."

A few years into Mom's teaching career, something was starting to happen to her. Grandma Ella said she should have paid more attention to the changes, or even talked directly to my mother about them, but Grandma had no idea what was unfolding within Mom.

Mom had begun taking Valium for her nerves. She complained about being anxious, but thought the feelings were a consequence of how seriously she took her job. At the same time she was experiencing anxiety, she was also excited. She knew

Dad was coming home soon, and they would be able to start their life together.

My father returned from the army, and my parents married. It was June 5, 1956, and their dreams were coming true. They were on their way toward the future.

They started by renting a farm near Burwell. They continued to work and save money until they could purchase a farm of their own.

Eventually, they put a down payment on a farm in Arcadia, Nebraska. Mom began teaching just a few miles from their new home. Dad began by planting corn and alfalfa. Quickly, he expanded his operation to include cattle, hogs, and chickens. Dad was a brilliant man. He was good at business. Life was unfolding nicely for the two of them.

Starting a family was on their minds, and one year later, I was born. The life they dreamed of seemed to be falling into place.

Mom's mind was in the genius range. Her education and faculties for memorization were considered to be off the charts. She was an amazing teacher, but teaching was taking an enormous toll on her. My father's work ethic was incredible; he was growing the farm in record speed, and it was making them a good living. And so, one day he asked my mom why she didn't quit teaching to help him on the farm. "We will do fine and raise our family," he said. Mom's stress had been increasing, and my father always had her best interests at heart, so she trusted his conviction that she should quit her job and stay at home.

In retrospect, it's easy to see that Mom's mind needed regular stimulation. Boredom grew in her like a sickness. She told her mother she didn't like staying at home. The farmwork was physical, and she put in long days, but she needed to work her mind as well as her body.

Instead, Mom was relegated to taking care of the household and looking after five hundred laying hens. Every week, she put eggs in an egg washer and took them into town to sell to the local grocery store for a little spending money. Dad continued growing our farm with more hogs and cattle. He purchased more land, and outwardly, everything seemed to be progressing well.

I was over three years old when my folks welcomed my baby brother. My grandma, who was staying to help for a while, encouraged Mom to let me hold him. I am not sure if it was my mother just being nervous, or if she was starting to change inside, but something was going on. There was a venomous look she sometimes gave me, though she said nothing at all. It put a scare into my body, like an angry northern winter wind blowing right through me, right into my heart. Even at that young age, I recognized the feeling of emotional betrayal. This began a disconnect between my mother and me that would shroud my heart and mind, and threaten to separate us long into adulthood.

Around this time, I began to seek surrogate mother figures. Sometimes, I was lucky enough to find one.

My favorite day of the week was Sunday. On Sundays, I would race up the cement steps, grab the big latch, and open the door to the church. The smell of the old building hit my nose as soon as I took a deep breath. Calmness washed over me as I looked at the colored windows, Jesus's cross, and the pews lined with Bibles. The bell would chime its deep, loud dong, signifying that it was time for Sunday school. The other kids would come running with me: down a narrow stairway, through a long hall, and to an open door where stood our smiling teacher.

"Please sit down, children." I could smell cookies on the dish in front of us. Our table was in the shape of a big circle. Every week, her same soft pink sweater draped over the table's only larger chair. She read us stories that I found captivating. The gentle way she spoke, and her kind reactions to our endless questions—the way she never lost patience when all our hands were up at once—was exactly what I needed from an adult back then.

"Karen, would you like to pass out the cookies?" Just hearing my name was enough to make me feel important. "Everyone, it's time for all of you to draw a picture of what you learned today." Then the bell would ring again, and my heart would sink that it was over. I watched the other kids find their parents. I waited for my teacher's warm hand to hold mine as we went upstairs together. At the foyer, I could see Mom's dark blue eyes, her face scowling.

"Evelyn, you have such a nice little girl here," my teacher said, touching my shoulder.

"Yes, she's special, all right."

I looked up at Mom, and my stomach ached.

"I will see you next week," I whispered under my breath as I got into the car, staring up at the old church, and tugging at the fingertips of my white gloves.

My father must have recognized my need for a companion because one day, he came into the house with a little puppy for me. I named her Coco. As she licked my face, I could feel how warm she was. I buried my nose in her fur. She smelled so good. Her paws were so little, and she only had a stub for a tail. Coco was an adorable cocker spaniel, and she was all mine. As I pulled away from wanting to help Mom with the new baby, Coco and I became inseparable.

STARTING TO LOSE MOM

om was extremely close to both her father and grandfather, but she was definitely a daddy's girl. Grandma used to say Mom took losing her grand-dad very, very hard, but "thank God she still had her daddy." The day her father died broke my mother in half.

Mom's brother called and told her to come to their folks' farm right away. Dad helped Mom get my brother and me into the car, and we took off. Mom was crying uncontrollably. The sound was devastating.

For days before the funeral, an endless throng of people came in and out of the house. They brought all kinds of food. All the grown-ups gathered in the kitchen. We were told to go play. I had to use the bathroom. The door was half-open as though no one was in there. I pushed it open and froze mid-step. There was my mom. She was sitting on the toilet with the lid down. She looked up and glared at me without saying a word. I couldn't move, and I couldn't get a sound out of my mouth. I just turned and ran to my bedroom. I shut the door behind me, sat on a chair by the window, and watched the people come and go. I forgot all about needing to use the restroom.

Grandpa was gone. At his funeral, I stared at his body in the casket and thought of the times I had sat on his lap, and how he somehow got me to eat peas. He was a quiet, gentle, soft-spoken man. I asked my uncle if I could touch Grandpa.

I heard my mother's reply, "No, don't take her up to the casket."

I didn't understand why. My uncle took me to him despite my mom's protests. He lifted me up, and I softly touched Grandpa's hand. I told my uncle that Grandpa was cold and that we should get him a blanket for heaven.

After the funeral, our house was very quiet. For days, no one said anything to me, and I had to find ways to occupy myself.

I noticed my mother started behaving differently in the afternoons. Dad would return to his work outside, and Mom would put my brother down for a nap. Then, Mom would take to her chair by the phone, where she would listen to other people's conversations on the party line, or she would lie down on the couch in the living room and fall asleep.

I took advantage of these moments by sneaking off to play in my mother's closet. Mom had a little, four-drawer, dresser-like cabinet in the corner of her closet. She used it for her underwear and bras. I pulled out the top drawer, and under her silk panties I discovered a disk that contained pills. It was pink and rotated inside the packaging. I pushed out a few pills and turned the dial a couple of times. Having entertained myself with that, I went on to play with Mom's high heels, enjoying the smell of perfume that clung to her dresses. Mom was so depressed after the loss of her dad, she wasn't even aware of my closet mischief. I don't know whether I helped cause it, but nine months later, we had a new baby sister.

Grandma came, longer this time, to help care for the new baby. Mom wasn't functioning well in the home. The daily chores of having three kids seemed to take all her energy. The pile of laundry in the bathroom had gotten almost as tall as I was.

Mom didn't make time to be alone with any of us; there wasn't "quality time." I would sometimes wander into the kitchen, where my grandmother seemed always to be cooking. She would let me help and started teaching me the art of Bohemian and Polish cooking. The aromas of her cuisine would carry all through the house as though you could eat the air.

Even though Mom was usually in the room with her, they wouldn't be speaking. Grandma kept quiet. Mom sat in the kitchen nook, staring out the window. You could always find her here. In the mornings, Mom had her hair in little rollers with a white pick stuck in each one so they wouldn't fall out. I never saw her without makeup. Her face was turned away from me, and I could see the line where her makeup stopped right on her jawbone. She always wore dark lipstick, but nothing on her eyes. When she wasn't looking at me, I thought her deep blue eyes and thick eyebrows were pretty. Mom always made sure to dress nicely, apart from one thing: it didn't matter if she was wearing shorts or pants—she always had on short nylon socks with shoes that had a tall, chunky heel. So many times, I wanted to tell her how ugly that looked.

Sometimes I looked at her, and I could smell her rose perfume. In these moments, I wanted to touch her arm, to lean in for the hug I'd never get. Instead, I turned around and left her staring out the window.

Time passed. Mom began to have moments of confusion, fear, and uncertainty. Being young, I couldn't intellectually understand what was happening, but I could watch and feel, and I knew that my mother wasn't in a good place.

I began spending more time squirreled away in my mother's closet. It became my safe place. I touched everything: the soft flannel of Mom's pink-and-white pajamas, her incredible pink robe, which felt like silk on my arms when I tried it on. I would make my way to the very back of the closet where it was almost too dark to see. There, on a hanger, was my favorite dress of all. It looked like it was made for a queen. The brilliant colors of pink, blue, black, and light green. I would put my head in the bottom of the dress to come up into it. I'd slip my arms through the sleeveless shoulders. I had hidden a pair of high heels—bright red, that I never saw Mom wear—to help me get into the dress. I would step in and my toes would almost go through the open toe of the shoe. Then I would try to walk. I had to be quiet because the floor was wood, and I didn't want anyone to hear the heel slide against it. I shuffled as softly as I could into the open part of the closet, where I'd grab each side of the dress and lift. A hidden part of the dress would open up, revealing a black insert that looked like an unfolded fan. I was too little to make it twirl, but when I closed my eyes, I could picture the dress flying outward like Cinderella's in the storybooks. I never stayed in the closet too long. I feared getting caught. I hung up the dress and turned to leave, but it was so dark that I tripped over all the shoes and fell over, hitting my head hard on a bottle.

I didn't dare reach up and pull the string to turn on the lightbulb, so I couldn't read what the bottle said. Still, I wanted to know what it was. I decided to unscrew the cap. I inhaled deeply, and the smell was so strong it stung as it went up my nose. I stuck my finger in the neck of the bottle and tried to taste it. As the taste touched my tongue, I started to gag. I hurried and screwed the cap back on. I was puzzled, but raced out of there. It seemed like the aroma was following me.

One night, I could hear my folks' voice coming up the vent in my bedroom. I got out of bed and pressed my ear to listen. Dad was questioning her about drinking. Their voices were getting louder like they were in an argument. I couldn't really hear clearly, so I got back in bed and pulled the covers up to my neck. I closed my eyes and thought about what Mom could have done to upset Dad.

Then, suddenly, I could hear them clearly. "Something is wrong; something is happening to my mind," Mom was saying. She was crying loudly to my father.

Coco, my dear dog, was lying beside me. She raised her head and looked at me. I told her I was scared. I wasn't getting hugs from my mom anymore, and there were no more good-night kisses, either. I told Coco I was sad. I wept softly into her coat, the warmth of my dog soothing me until I fell asleep.

During this time, my siblings and I often played outside. Outside always felt better, safer than the house. My brother had a little red tractor and wagon. He would put hard kernels of corn in the wagon and, from his knees, push it down the driveway. One day, we found my little sister sitting in a hole by our lilac bush. She was playing in the dirt, making mud pies that she was actually eating. My brother and I should have stopped her, but we were little, and so instead, we laughed. Her mouth was dripping with mud.

Then, I heard the screen door slam. Seconds later, I felt the skin on my arm twisting.

"You goddamn dumbbell! Why aren't you watching your sister?" Mom yanked me across the yard, dragging me over grass and dirt patches.

"I didn't do anything! I didn't!" I screamed. I could see the lilac tree. Then the hole my sister was eating from. I closed my lips as tightly as I could. I wouldn't eat dirt.

"You . . . God . . . Damn . . . Dumb . . . Bell," she repeated, striking me between each syllable for effect. It didn't matter. I wouldn't swallow mud. Then she let go. There was stillness. My arm burned where she'd gripped it. I lay on my stomach, listening for movement. There wasn't a sound. I turned my head slightly. Her eyes were piercing. I scrambled away, running before I was even upright. I ran until I couldn't run anymore. I ran to the cow pen where we had a hydrant. It was used for hooking up hoses to wash equipment or give water to the animals. I tried lifting the handle again and again. It wasn't budging. Finally, it gave way, and water came shooting down. I gagged and spat, grabbing my tongue with my fingers, scraping the grains of dirt from my mouth.

The house looked so far away from where I stood. It seemed like everything was dark around the house, like it was standing alone in a mist or fog. At that moment, I thought I would never go back inside.

That was the first time Mom hit me. The days were getting scary. Mom was yelling and blaming me for things I didn't understand. She would let the screen door slam; that was my cue. I'd think, *Oh God, which way is she coming?* Looking right at me, she'd raise her hand and point a finger at me. I knew she would hurt me, but I couldn't move. I stood waiting, stiffening, and praying. *Don't hit me. Please, don't hit me.*

"Can you see the holes?" she demanded. "Can you?"

I glanced at the siding of the house, where she was pointing. The paint was chipping, but I couldn't see any holes. She ranted about bullet holes in the house. I was beginning to realize these were bullet holes only she could see.

Still, I knew better than to tell her there were no holes. So, I nodded.

"You play on the east side of the house with your brother and sister," she told me. "Are you so damn stupid to not know they will shoot at you on the west side?"

I couldn't comprehend what was happening. I was like the stray kittens roaming around the farm. It doesn't matter to the kitten that its mama swats it; the kitten keeps bowing its head and coming back for more. I couldn't quit going near Mom, even though I knew her swat would come.

I decided to try to win her affection in other ways, such as by helping in the kitchen. I decided to get all the dirty dishes done for her. I wasn't sure where Mom was in the house, but I filled the sink with hot soapy water and started in. There were a lot of pots and pans from the fried chicken, mashed potatoes, and gravy she'd made in the cast-iron skillets. I scraped as hard as I could with the steel wool pad. I knew I couldn't leave any trace of old food.

My hands were red and wrinkled as I neared the end. Finally, I got to the last pan—the cast-iron nightmare. I could hardly lift it. When I put it in the sink, it slipped out of my hands and dropped into the water like a heavy sack of potatoes. The water cascaded over the edge onto the floor. I cringed and grabbed a tea towel to sop up the water. I listened, hearing only silence. *Thank God,* I thought, *Mom must not have heard the commotion.*

I finished cleaning the skillet. It took both my hands and all my strength to lift it out of the water and onto the draining tray. I'd barely let go when her hand clutched my wrist.

"You think you're smart? I don't know why you turned the handles that direction."

I looked at her face. Her eyebrows looked like they were touching one another. I couldn't see my wrist, but my hand was deep, reddish blue with such an ache. I didn't understand her criticism. The handles? What was wrong with the handles?

A week or so had gone by, and one afternoon, Mom told me to tidy up the entry room off the front porch. We all kept our shoes there so we didn't track dirt into the house. I wanted to do a good job. I moved all the shoes and took the rug outside, shaking it to free it of dirt. I proceeded to stack the shoes in perfect rows.

When I finished, I went outside to play with my cats. The day seemed okay. Later, I came in because I was getting hungry. I couldn't believe my eyes. The shoes were spread all over the porch like someone had thrown them everywhere. As I looked around, Mom greeted me. She grabbed me by my shoulders and turned me around fast. She shoved me hard in the middle of my back.

"When you point the shoes the right way, you can have something to eat."

I was lost. I couldn't figure out what she was saying. I started to cry. What did it matter which way the shoes pointed?

"What's the trouble here?" It was the kind voice of my dad. I thought I was saved. I couldn't say what the trouble was because I was afraid Mom would hear me. I just stood there, waiting for Dad to fix it. Suddenly, Mom was there, too, putting the shoes on the rug.

"She needs to finish her job."

I looked at Dad.

"Well, get it done and come eat," he said.

I looked at the way she put the first pair so I knew which way the rest of the shoes needed to go. When I finished, I went inside and sat down at the table. Everyone was eating. I took a bite of meat and looked at Mom. I felt as though her eyes were staring right through me, and I couldn't eat anymore. I asked to be excused. I went upstairs and hid under my bed. I thought I was fine. I thought I was safe.

Then I heard someone racing up our narrow stairway. The wood stairs made a loud creaking sound, so I could tell someone was coming. My bedspread lifted, and there was Mom's face. I was so startled I let out a loud scream.

"You think you're safe every time your dad is around? Get out from under there! Now!"

I couldn't move; I didn't want to come out. There was a sudden stabbing feeling in my side, then my leg, and my arm. I cried, "Please! Stop!"

I saw her face as she continued to poke me hard with the end of the green mop. I knew I had to crawl out. I made it partway and felt my arm almost leaving my body as she pulled me up, bending my body so she could hit my butt over and over again with her open hand. Maybe it was her hand that hurt when she finally stopped. I ran as fast as I could down the stairs. I went sliding down some of them, missing a few, but going as fast as my legs could go. I ran outside, hearing the screen door slam behind me. I raced to the grove of thick trees we had near the house. I had a favorite cottonwood tree that I could crawl up into, way up to the middle where no one could see me. As I took a deep breath, I looked at my leg and arm to see how bad the marks were this time.

One morning at the breakfast table, my brother accidentally spilled my milk. It splashed across the table, splattering down the leg of the table and pooling onto the floor. Mom whirled, eyed me with her cold stare, and yelled my name.

There was no time to defend myself. I knew it would be useless, anyway, since she always blamed me. I ran up the stairs and crawled under my bed, my heart racing. I heard Mom's footsteps, heavy on the stairs.

My door creaked open, and I heard her dragging the broom behind her. I was petrified of my mother then. I didn't know who she was anymore. I didn't recognize at all the woman who was supposed to love me.

She dipped down and raised the blanket of my bed, her cold eyes chilling me. She slid the broom underneath, poking my leg.

"Come out," she ground out between clenched teeth. "Come out and get your punishment."

Reluctantly, I crawled out. She grabbed my arm, hard, whirled me around, and laid four quick swats on my behind. The spanking didn't hurt nearly as much as her anger, which felt like a living thing in the room, a dangerous thing.

I was losing love for my mom. It was being replaced with feelings of fear and anger. I wondered what Mom was so scared of. *Who were these people she kept talking about—the people shooting at the house and trying to hurt us?* I would look around the farmyard and wonder where they were, and why I couldn't see them. Sometimes, I would stand close to the siding of the house and stare at every seam. *Where were the bullet holes?* Holes that only she seemed to see. I just knew I had to stay out of her way as much as I could. I started hiding for hours in different places. The big closet in our dining room was the best. I would sneak in there and slide the door shut. From inside, I could hear every noise and tell exactly where Mom was at all times. Sometimes, I would fall asleep and be in there for hours. No one ever found my safe place.

Mom belonged to a group called Rebecca Lodge. The ladies would meet once a month. It was a warm, spring day the one time my mother said I could come with her. I ran upstairs to my room and put on my favorite plaid dress. When I came down, I went into the bathroom as Mom was spraying her hair one more time to hold it in place. She turned and looked at me and picked up her favorite bottle of perfume.

"Come here. I will put a little squirt on you so you smell good, too."

I wanted to hug her, but I just stood there watching the spray coming out of the bottle, feeling the coolness hit my skin. When we arrived, I looked around the room. All the ladies wore pretty dresses with matching earrings. Mom had on a blue dress, one of my favorites. All the ladies had tall high heels that matched the color of their dresses. The chatter and laughter blended into a loud echo that filled the room. Mom smiled the whole time. Everything was magical there. Driving home with her in that state felt like pure happiness to me. But her expression changed the nearer we got to our driveway.

As we pulled up to the house, the sudden slam on the brakes jerked my head forward. Mom's eyes were glued to the house. Her body looked frozen.

"Get in the house."

I could hardly open the car door. I followed her as she walked swiftly inside.

"Go to your room."

Tightness seized my body. I took off running to my room. I stopped and hid behind the door to the stairs. Peeking around the corner, I could see Mom holding the phone.

"I know who you are! Are you in our house? Have you been here today? You don't fool me!" I watched her pace back and forth as the phone cord stretched out across the kitchen.

Who was she talking to? She slammed the phone down and began walking right toward me. I slid backward, turned, and darted upstairs, as quickly and quietly as I could. Once in my room, I hid in my closet, trying to catch my breath.

When Dad came in from outside, Mom tried to tell him about the conspiracies against him and how the world was out to get him. His face deepened with confusion and frustration. His voice got louder. "You don't make any sense! What's the matter with you?"

I endlessly watched my mother, but in no way did I think she was becoming mentally ill. I didn't even know what that meant. I was beginning to feel insecure. I hated when she'd stare at me with such coldness in her eyes; I constantly turned my head away from her to avoid eye contact—anything to spare myself from that stare. Most of the time, Mom would be in the kitchen cooking, but she was spending more and more time just sitting on a chair by the phone, listening to all the people talking on the party line. Sometimes I could hear a person say, "I know someone is listening to our phone call. Please hang up." Mom would slide her hand over the mouthpiece of the phone and listen still.

Only on Saturday nights, my parents' date night, was my mom's behavior reliably "normal." They would take us with them to National Hall, a cinder block structure filled with polka and laughter. It was in the middle of nowhere.

Time slowed as I watched my parents twirl in love, the twinkling lights falling softly across Mom's face as she fell into Dad's arms, a smile as wide as the mountain sky. When they danced at Jungmann Hall, another country dance hall, there were mattresses in the back room so the kids could sleep while their parents danced the night away. My little brother would sometimes hold on to my parents' hands and dance between them in a group circle. My little sister would run up and down the hall with the other children her size. There were a few girls my age, and we connected instantly. We would dance together and giggle about all sorts of things. When the band paused to rest, all the parents bought us kids chocolate pop and hot dogs. The entire hall smelled like hot dogs. The music and the grown-ups' laughter made it feel so exciting.

Sometimes, instead of taking us with them, my parents would drop us off at Grandma Ella's house. Our cousins would often be there as well. When my grandmother was done watching Lawrence Welk, she'd teach us how to play pitch. We would sit around her oblong kitchen table, where she had a little white bowl filled with peppermint candy. Whoever won the game got one piece of candy. We were resilient little creatures of habit. It didn't take long before we'd all try cheating so we could win our candy prize. My grandma was no fool. Anyone she caught cheating would have to sit out one game for punishment. When we were done playing cards, we'd head to the living room. Each of us had a pillow, and Grandma would cover us up and turn the lights out.

On one particular Saturday night, as I was lying on the couch at my grandma's, I heard her front door open. This was followed by the loud voices of my dad and uncle.

"I don't know what's wrong. She's been doing this more every day."

I felt his fingers pressing on my back. "Get up. Time to go."

I picked the pillow up off the floor and put it back on the couch. Dad had my little sister in his arms. She didn't want to wake up. As all of us were walking into the dark night, hanging on to the stair railing so we wouldn't miss a step, I could hear Grandma saying good-bye. My uncle was getting his two girls into his car with my aunt. I noticed Mom sitting in our front seat. She was staring at me through the car window. I could see the steam of her breath hit the glass. As I grabbed the door handle to open the car door, the loudest scream came from inside the car.

"Get in the car, you damn dumbbell!" My hand went weak. I could barely open the door. I wasn't sure what was going on. I got in the back seat, and Dad put my siblings in from the other side. The seat was so cold. I worked to piece together what was happening. I looked over at my siblings. They were leaning their heads on one another, sleeping. I leaned my head on the car door, but I couldn't sleep. Rocks from the gravel road struck the underside of the car. I stared at the dark sky, looking out at thousands of stars.

SHE IS GONE

W e were playing outside when my uncle and aunt drove into the yard. Grandma Ella was with them. Grandma never learned to drive, so she had to catch a ride anytime she wanted to see us. This time, she entered the house carrying a big black suitcase. I didn't know what she was doing. Mom was crying. My uncle was holding her hand, saying, "It will be okay, sis, you just need some help." Dad and my aunt and uncle all left in the car with Mom. Just like that, she was gone.

Grandma said she would be staying with us to help out for a while until Mom felt well enough to come home. It was such a strange feeling. I loved my grandmother, but the reason for her visit confused me. I missed my mom, yet was glad for the reprieve from her mounting physical and emotional abuse. I was mixed up and didn't really know what to feel.

I overheard Grandma Ella on the phone. She was telling my other grandma, Grandma Mary, they had diagnosed Mom with severe mania and a deep case of schizophrenia. Dad and Grandma tried their best to keep the household running normally. Grandma would make sure the meals were ready when Dad came home from work. They chatted about the day, but no one said a word about Mom. It was like she had left the planet. I wanted to ask about her, but I wasn't entirely sure what to say.

Weeks went by, or maybe even months. Dad told me Mom would be better soon and would be coming home. Dad could tell I was unsure of what was happening, so he asked me if I'd like to go see her. I was so excited and happy to go. We left for the hospital the next morning. I don't know why, but I thought the hospital would be near us. I kept asking why Mom was so far away.

I was struck by how large the buildings were, as I had never been in a big city before. I wondered how we would even find Mom in such a huge place.

We entered the hospital by stepping on a black mat that made the doors open automatically. I looked around. It seemed like there wasn't a ceiling. I saw stairs going everywhere. How were we going to find Mom?

I held Dad's hand as he pulled me toward a desk where a woman was sitting. There was a huge phone with flashing lights on her desk. Every which way, people were walking by in the same-colored pants and tops. I listened as Dad said Mom's name. It was so different to hear our last name spoken there, in that place. I saw some chairs to sit on.

It wasn't like a modern waiting room; there were no books or magazines, no corner full of well-worn toys. Dad told me to sit down, that he would be right back to get me. The woman at the desk watched me. I felt like I was frozen. I didn't dare make a sound. I just put my hands under my legs and waited. I kept looking for Dad. The room smelled like the rubbing alcohol we kept beneath our bathroom sink.

Dad returned and held my hand as we went upstairs in an elevator. It was the first time I'd been in an elevator, and I couldn't believe all the noises and buttons. We walked down a long hall and went into a room.

There is no question that electroconvulsive therapy, or ECT, was benefiting patients then, but there is also a lot of evidence from that period showing the ECT, and the threat of it, were used in mental hospitals to control difficult patients and to maintain order on wards. ECT was also physically dangerous when first developed. There is no question that ECT causes some memory loss, particularly of events near the time of the treatment. Permanent long-term memory loss does occur, and it is uncertain how common it is. Many clinicians believe it to be exceedingly rare based on their experience treating patients over the years.[1]

I had no idea what electric shock treatments were, or that Mom was receiving two such treatments per day, and would continue to do so until she received a total of fifty. Shock treatments had become legal, but only in large hospitals like this one in Omaha.

I remember Mom's weak smile when she saw me. Her hair wasn't combed. She looked tired even though it was early afternoon. She was still wearing pajamas. She looked sad, and apart from saying she really wanted to go home, she was quiet. Dad told her it wouldn't be long, that her treatment was almost complete. I may have been little, but I could tell she was unhappy and scared, too.

While we were in the room, a nurse said she was sorry about Evelyn's teeth. I didn't know my mother wore dentures.

---

1   Jonathan Sadowsky, "Electroconvulsive Therapy: A History of Controversy, but Also of Help," *The Conversation,* January 13, 2017.

The nurse told Dad they had forgotten to remove them before a treatment, and the teeth had shattered in her mouth. Mom didn't currently have any teeth. Dad said the hospital should pay for new dentures. The nurse agreed, and Mom started to cry.

I don't know if it was because she was happy to hear about new teeth coming or because she was sad that her teeth were missing. I desperately wanted to give her some that day, as a present. I looked at Mom the whole time. I loved the pink robe she was wearing. It was the one she wore to make our breakfast every morning.

Dad said it was time for the two of us to go home. I was confused why Mom had to stay. Mom looked fine. She just needed her hair combed and to get dressed. I gave her a hug, but she felt different in my arms. I don't know why; she just did, like something was missing. I noticed she didn't smell of roses like she did at home. I looked at her lips as they seemed sunken in her mouth. As we were leaving the room, I looked back and saw Mom's eyes full of tears as she watched us go.

For a long time after her shock treatments, Mom was quiet. She was like a lost, numb shell of her former self. I watched her personality dissolve. Her humor disappeared, as did bits and pieces of her memory. Mom would remember one person's birthday, but not another's. She had to be reminded of certain dates, and it bothered her immensely. The parts of her memory that disappeared remained gone forever. Mom came home, but parts of her personality—things that made her unique— never did.

LAUGHTER AND FEAR

M y brother was a typical boy. One afternoon, Mom, my little sister, and I were standing in the kitchen when he walked in holding a short stick with a snake curling around it. Mom screamed like I had never heard her scream before. She went into hysterics. The snake fell off the stick, slithering fast over the floor and under the couch. Mom shrieked for us all to get up on the couch.

It so happened that the gas man who filled up our big fuel tanks for the farm equipment was just outside the window.

"Karen, you jump down and go get the gas man. Ask him to come in here to help us!"

I did, and he came in. I could tell by his contained smirk that he wanted to laugh. He moved one of the sections of the couch and grabbed the snake, taking it outside. Mom was grateful and thanked him repeatedly for saving us. My brother stood there giggling. I thought Mom would hit him. I was waiting for her to erupt, but she just walked off.

In the moment, I did what I was told. I didn't protest or even pause to question Mom's directive. The moment called for action, and so I leaped from the couch, and raced to the door quickly. What bugged me the most wasn't the snake. It was the feeling that lingered long after the moment ended. I didn't feel chosen—it wasn't like being a kid in school when the teacher asks one lucky student to come erase the blackboard. I felt sacrificed. I always wondered why, without a moment's hesitation, Mom picked me to get down off the safety of the couch. It may, of course, simply been because I was the oldest. But I had so little faith in her desire to protect me, and now, that strikes me as the most biting thing of all.

Mom put her arms around my brother and sister to see if they were okay, but she did not put her arms around me. I looked at her and thought, *You don't care about me. You didn't care if the snake bit me.* I felt unwanted. I had an ache in my chest that wouldn't go away. Later, I punched my brother and told him it was all his fault. He didn't seem to care what happened; he was just a boy having fun.

Some days would drag, while others went by so fast. The drudge of not knowing how Mom was going to be each day weighed hard on me. Sometimes I would look at the gravel road in front of our house and watch the dust rolling high in the sky when someone drove past.

The best moments were those when the passing pickup truck turned up our drive. That meant my uncle was coming. I loved when he came over. His presence meant I would have a safe day. He was a riot, and I could tell he loved us. We were his sister's kids.

He had also grown up with our dad. They were high school buddies and went into the army together. I would get to stay with his family sometimes for a week in the summer, and I always looked forward to those trips. Life was different at their place.

My uncle knew how to bring laughter to us in a way that my parents did not. We often went over there in the spring, when the baby calves needed to be worked so they could go to pasture with their mothers for the summer. "Working" meant the calves would be branded, vaccinated, and castrated so they would grow to be steers instead of bulls. This way they could be sold for meat. My uncle always did the castrating. My cousins and siblings and I would watch and help, handing supplies to our dad, our uncle, or the other guys who were helping out.

At one point, my uncle threw a set of calf testicles on top of the barrel of hot flames where the branding irons were kept. We could hear them sizzling. Once cooked, he grabbed them, put them in his mouth, and swallowed them in front of us. We were stunned. Our jaws dropped. We couldn't speak. He threw another pair onto the barrel. And just as we thought he was going to eat this pair, too, he snatched them up and started toward us. We all screamed and took off running. He kept yelling, "If I catch one of you, I'll make you swallow these nuts!" My uncle started laughing so hard he couldn't run after us anymore. It was so good for everyone's souls to laugh that hard. I enjoyed this slice of normalcy for just a brief moment in our lives.

I loved it when my folks said I could go stay at my aunt and uncle's, and even though the visits were short, I was able to escape the stresses of being in my own home. My nervous stomach went away. The constant fear went away. The lack of self-worth went away.

I would gaze at my aunt and uncle and listen to how they spoke to each other. There was no talk of people firing at the house, or of people who were wearing the wrong color. No one said you had to play on a certain part of the yard so you wouldn't get shot. Rather, their conversations were about doing chores, what the day had in store, and what time to have dinner.

One of the most important realizations I had at their house was that there wasn't any yelling or name-calling. They never hit their kids or told them they were dumb. It was a different kind of mothering. I couldn't help but compare. My mom had gone to the hospital for a long time, and even that had only "fixed her," made her someone who could smile and have fun, for a little while. But here at my uncle's place, while there was hard work, and my uncle was a driven farmer just like my dad, there was also fun.

My uncle had all of us kids take turns sitting on their small pony named Pepper. He put his hand on Pepper's rump, and the pony started bucking like crazy. It made us scream, and we were scared of falling off. My uncle laughed, which made us all laugh, watching each other trying to hang on when it was our turn.

During another stay, my aunt invited her niece from her side of the family. We were the same age, and I was happy to meet a new friend.

One evening, my aunt wanted us to take baskets and go gather all the eggs from the chicken house, where there were a couple of hundred laying hens.

Somehow, the cruel idea arose to throw an egg at a chicken and see if we could hit it. The only blessing was that we were terrible shots and couldn't hit anything. Needless to say, the game went on until we had managed to break almost all the eggs. Not surprisingly, when our aunt caught us, she was very upset. To my amazement, there wasn't name-calling or hitting. Mom would've done both; my aunt did neither.

Instead, my aunt looked at us for a while and then said, "You both need to be taught a lesson." She took the little purse I had brought with me and took the other niece's Barbie doll and said, "I will put these up, and you don't get them until you go home," which was days away. We sat on the outside steps, and I told the other little girl that I was waiting for the beating and the name-calling. The stare she returned to me showed she had no comprehension of what I was saying.

The rest of my stay went smoothly, and my aunt didn't bring the matter up again. We did fun things, and it was a great visit. My aunt and uncle had rules and chores, but we loved being there. When it came time to go home, it was like a switch flicked inside me. I quit talking and retreated into my own spinning mind as I prepared to go back to my "normal."

I was always looking for things to do so I could stay far away from the house. I loved it when Dad said it was time to get the horses from the pasture and saddle them for cattle work. He would tell me the day before, because it took a half day to get them in.

I went down with my bucket of grain, and they followed me right up until I almost had them in the corral, and then, just like that, they took off. They bucked and galloped as though they were laughing at me, saying, "Catch me if you can." I would get my bucket and start all over. It would take me hours to coax them back again. I really didn't mind, because it kept me busy all day. I didn't have a care in the world on those days. I enjoyed the smells of wild flowers and felt the peace of the wind.

It was so hard for me to walk up to the house to go inside. The prospect always made me feel weak. *Just get in the house and run to your room,* I told myself.

Sometimes I would do something unintentional that would aggravate my mother's ill feelings toward me. There were days things were quiet. Then, for no reason at all, a flaming verbal attack would come on. I'd suddenly be the target of her vitriol. Sometimes, I wondered if this was the only attention I'd get from my mother. Other times, I'd think being ignored was actually better.

One day, my brother and I were playing outside in the trees where there was a stack of old lumber. We got into a fight. I grabbed a board off the stack and hit him on top of his head with it. A split second later, I saw something shooting out of his head. It was spraying upward. I couldn't tell what it was until it hit his hand. My God, it was blood! I panicked. I looked at the board, and I could see there was a nail sticking out of it. I didn't know what to do.

The first thing I said was, "Don't tell Mom!" I tried putting my hand on his head to stop the bleeding. He started screaming and took off running to the house. I started to follow and then turned and hid by a big tree. I knew what my punishment was going to be.

Mom screamed so loudly I could hear her fear. "You come here right now!" I felt sick to my stomach, but I knew I had to go.

The first hit felt like my head smashed into a wall. The second sent my head wavering from side to side. The third stung, and by the fourth, I couldn't feel anything anymore. I could only hear her ringing words in my ears, "You make me so mad! You're such a damn dumb kid! Don't ever let me catch you doing this again!" It finally ended, and I stood on the step. I knew I had hurt my brother, but all I could register was that my mother had called me stupid.

Later, when my brother and I were alone, I told him to show me his head. I could see a dried blood spot. I was relieved it wasn't still bleeding and realized then that it had been a superficial wound. I tried to figure out how I could have done that to him. Why would I hit him with a board? In that guilt, I realized how much I loved him. Was I a damn dumbbell? Maybe.

ROLLER COASTER

I was struggling to make sense of the relationship between my mother and me, and of the daily life of our household. Why did the good times never last?

Almost every Saturday, we would go to the little town of Ord because it had more stores than our town. Normally, we would go with Mom while she did her shopping; other times, Dad would let me go with him. He loved this place called Eddie's Pool Hall, where he could have a couple of beers, shoot some pool, and visit with the friends he had known his whole life. I loved going with Dad and watching everyone there. He let me have Cherry Coke, and I noticed how different it was to be in a bar with Dad instead of Mom. I didn't feel embarrassed or scared. I could see the happiness on the rugged faces of the old farmers.

When Mom came in and announced she was finished with her shopping, we left hurriedly—Dad never wanted to linger.

Next, we would head straight for Douthit's Diner, a restaurant close to the pool hall. They had the best hot beef sandwiches. The aroma of homemade rolls made the restaurant deliciously cozy. There was no place in the world I preferred to go.

Reflecting back all these years later, I now recognize why this time was so special. We were all together, eating, loving, feeling like we had a beautiful family connection. But I knew it wouldn't last. How could each day be so different? One was filled with joy, and the next was crazy.

Without warning, the Saturday outings stopped, and there were no more family lunches at the diner. Even as a child, I knew something was wrong. I could feel the vibe in our home becoming heavy. Mom began talking more often about strangers trying to hurt the family. It went from once or twice a week to nearly two or three times per day. I could tell Dad was bothered by all of this and didn't want anyone else to witness her behavior.

Once in a while, in these early years, we took fishing trips to Canada with my uncle's family. Dad and Mom's brother went to an island to fish while the rest of us stayed at the cabin. Occasionally, Mom gave us treats such as rides on a small plane that took off and landed on the water, but much of the day, she just stared into space.

One evening, the groundkeeper's daughter's pet owl was killed. Someone had wrung its neck and left its head separated from its body. When we went to the lodge for breakfast the next morning, his daughter was crying. I was devastated for her, looking at her owl and the feathers all around.

"They're here to hurt people, too," Mom said. I looked at her and couldn't understand what she meant. I looked at the little girl. She looked back at me, and we just stared at each other for a moment, as if we both knew we were confused and hurting about life.

Later that day, she was sitting on the lodge steps by herself. I went to her and asked her if they figured out what or who had killed her owl. She said her dad thought it was some local drunks that lived nearby. I told her how sorry I was and how much I loved animals. I came up with the idea to have a little funeral for her pet. We took some feathers and dug a little hole, and she said her good-bye. I never brought up my mother, nor did she. I was hoping she didn't hear what Mom had said.

Fall season was approaching. The first day of school finally arrived. I was scared to meet new kids. I put on my favorite plaid dress—the same dress I wore to Rebecca Lodge, and I walked down the long driveway from our house to wait by the mailbox for the big yellow school bus. I wondered what Mom would say to my teacher if I did anything wrong. I wondered if she would come to the school and yell at me in front of everyone. I had no idea this wasn't everyone's fear. I carried such nervousness inside, that when I stuck out my hand, it would lightly shake.

I couldn't believe it—the first day of school I spilled milk on my dress. When the teacher came to help me, I expected her to yell at me and tell me I was a dumbbell. I cowered before her. Instead, she was kind and thoughtful. When she asked me if I wanted my mom to come with a change of clothes, I quickly said no. I told her I would be okay. I stopped short of begging her not to call, of confessing my fear of doing anything that might upset my mother.

I loved school. It was my safe haven, a place where I was allowed to just be. The inability to identify and articulate my nervousness kept me closed off at school. I was quiet. When the bus driver dropped me off at our driveway, I kicked every rock and took as long as I could to get home. I wasn't in a hurry. Going home was the scariest part of the day. I was never sure what Mom would be like when I walked through the door. Sometimes, when I would walk in the house, Mom would be fixing supper and making really great meals. She was a wonderful cook. She would be so busy she didn't have time for me. On those days, I would just change my clothes and go play with my animals. Those days were good. Other times, I would come home to the stranger I didn't want to know.

One afternoon, I walked in the kitchen and felt the change immediately.

Mom had just finished drying a dish and she put it away. "Do you have any papers with you so I can see if you're a dumbbell?"

As she grabbed my schoolbag to go through it, she found one that didn't have an A on it. She crumpled it up and threw it away.

"You sure don't take after me. I don't know where you got your dumbness. Get out of here." I ran to my room. Sometimes I'd cry, sometimes not. But either way, a deep resentment started burning in my chest.

I looked for approval elsewhere. Often, I found it with my teachers. One teacher, Ms. Rosa Buck, was my favorite. I loved her so much, I didn't want to miss a single day of school in her class. At the end of the school year, there was an awards ceremony. Mrs. Buck got up and said my name, announcing my perfect attendance award. When I walked up to get my certificate, it seemed like there were hundreds of people in the audience, and they were all clapping for me. For a short period, though shy and confused, I was happy with myself. When I reached my teacher, she gave me the dearest, biggest hug. I needed to get to her every day for her hug; she was a surrogate for my mother's love.

Summertime was here again. I wasn't really aware that I was removing myself from connecting with my mom. I only knew that I couldn't get into trouble if I wasn't in the house.

Our farm was five miles from two little towns. Dad was always busy. I never saw him or the hired help until lunchtime, and then he would work until supper. I played in his shop or in the trees and watched him drive by on a tractor. I pretended I was talking to him and telling him what was on my mind, wondering what I was doing wrong to make Mom so angry with me.

After Mom fed us lunch, Dad would head back out for the afternoon.

"Come on. Let's get in the car," Mom would say, grabbing her tan purse. I hated hearing those words even though it was almost a daily event. She drove to a small town in the opposite direction of my school and the familiar shops. She didn't talk as she pulled up in front of the tavern. I had no idea what beer was, but that's what she ordered. To keep us quiet, she'd buy us each a pop.

I was so afraid to ride home in the car with Mom. The car would slide back and forth across the loose gravel. I watched out the window as the fence posts on the side of the road flew by. One time, Mom took a curve so hard that my door flew open. I could see the gravel road racing by so fast as the car door was swinging wildly and weeds were whipping against it from the side of the road. I felt her arm reach over to grab hold of me. My fear was so strong about falling out of the car I couldn't feel how tight Mom's grip was on my arm. I looked at Mom and down at her feet. Both her feet were pushing hard on the brake as she held the steering wheel with only one hand.

The car door slammed shut. I could smell the dust, and I could tell the car had stopped. Instantly, I felt hard, swift hits to my head. The words *goddamn dumbbell* had become as common as *good morning.* The constant berating hurt worse than the sting of her hand or the bumps on my head.

The next day when we headed to the bar, I sat in the back seat. I hated hearing Mom laughing with the bartender.

"You know, they are shooting at our house. People around Richard wear certain-colored clothes. He's so stupid he don't know how they're making a fool of him."

Then she'd laugh like she couldn't stop. I drank my pop silently. Dad wasn't stupid, but I didn't know how to protect him. The bartender just shook his head, always agreeing with Mom. His expression never changed. He just kept his head down and shook it back and forth. I think he put up with the ranting because she was a good customer. But at times, I'm sure he pitied us. He sometimes gave us candy. I wondered what he said about Mom after we left.

Sometimes, my siblings and I would stay inside and play on the bar's pool table, but most of the time, I took my brother and sister outside and we played on the curb. The town was so tiny, there wasn't much traffic. We entertained ourselves by drawing in the dirt and playing with rocks. I began caring more and more for my brother and sister. I was taking on family responsibilities quickly; childhood was fleeting.

Leaving the bar, we had no idea she was impaired or what danger she was putting us in. She always got us home, so we accepted our new routine without question. I wonder if Dad ever knew. We never talked about it. Sometimes in the evening, I would look at Dad at the supper table, wanting to tell him about it, but it was almost like Mom could read my mind. She grabbed my hair, yanked my head back, and said, "You'd better never tell your dad, or I will beat the shit out of you." I never said a word to Dad. Fear was my constant companion.

MY PATH

The neighbor lady would often take me to events and school functions. I liked being anywhere I could forget about the fear back home and just focus on having fun. Our neighbor had seven kids, and one day, a big storm came through the county, washing out the road in between our homes. One of the challenges of living on the farm was the unpredictability of the weather. The car was stuck, packed with all of us kids. I could smell something funny, and I started to get very sleepy. I lay down in the back, with my nose in the crack of the seat.

Sometime later, Dad was there pulling the car through the flooded road with his tractor chain hooked to it.

The next thing I knew, he was carrying me into the house. He laid me on the floor in the dining room. I have no idea how he found us, pulled the car out, and got us to our yard. I heard Dad yell, "She has carbon monoxide poisoning, and we are thirty-five miles to the nearest hospital!" Dad was on the phone. I could hear him, but I couldn't make out the words. I began rocking uncontrollably back and forth like a rag doll. I couldn't feel my dad's arms as he picked me up and carried me to the car. Even though it was still raining hard, Mom held me with my head out the window. I couldn't feel the rain hit my face, and I heard Dad say, "Keep her awake, no matter what!"

This incident happened at a time when I was aware that I was losing my mother. Yet in that moment, I could feel her physical love wrapped around me, and I could sense how important I was to her. I was confused, because when I was on the floor, I saw her just staring at me. I wanted her to help me, but she just stood there, not bothering to reach down to hold me or touch me. I wanted to cry out, "Mom, don't you want me? Am I going to die? Do you care?" Her mind was darkening, and her contempt for me was increasing once again. It seemed like love and compassion were about to wash away.

Feeling unwanted at home sometimes made school challenging for me. Being bullied as a "normal" little kid from a normal home is bad enough, but being degraded at home as well as at school has an exponential impact.

At recess, one little girl, a ringleader, decided to target me. She told all the other girls to hold hands and form a line, but not to hang on to my hand. They ran by me laughing and singing, "Don't let Karen hang on to us." I wasn't wanted at home, and now I wasn't wanted at school. I felt isolated.

There was only one other girl who also wasn't asked to join hands. I looked at her face as she was looking at mine. I noticed how quiet she was. I knew her from the school bus. She sat in the back. I smiled at her, and we became friends with an unspoken connection. I never asked Carol what her hurt was, but I knew no one played with her, either.

I was way too young to understand how feelings get projected, and I didn't know that being constantly nervous wasn't normal. I didn't know how to not feel lost and abandoned.

One afternoon at school, I was going down the slide at the playground. It was a very hot day, and the slide was made out of metal. I was wearing black-and-white, rubber-soled shoes—the old cheerleader oxfords.

I was excited to show my friend, Carol, what we could do.

"Watch! We can go down the slide squatting since the slide is so hot!" When I reached the bottom, my shoes stuck, and I was thrown into the air. Carol said I did a complete flip and came down on the corner of the metal slide, headfirst, hitting my mouth on the hard edge. I broke off one of my front permanent teeth almost to the gumline and chipped a big corner off the other front tooth. Carol reached down to pick me up off the dusty ground. It hurt so badly, I had my hands covering my mouth. As soon as I took my hands down and air hit it, pain raced through my face, consuming my whole head.

When the teacher came running to me and said she wanted to call my mother so she could come pick me up, I told her not to. I kept saying, "No! I will be fine. I'll ride the bus like I'm supposed to." No one at school knew what my homelife was like—the yelling and the beatings. My mouth hurt so badly. I was terrified as I rode the bus home. I kept my mouth shut. The nerve endings were alive, and I could feel them throbbing, almost like a heartbeat.

When I got home, I went straight to my room. As I walked past Mom, she told me that our neighbors had invited our family over for cards and food. I was told to change my clothes because we'd be leaving soon. I didn't know what to do.

"Why are you so quiet tonight?" Dad asked once we were in the car.

I turned my head toward the window so my brother and sister couldn't see me, and I said, "I don't know, I'm just tired." The pain was almost too much for me.

It was a beautiful evening, and when we arrived at our destination, all the kids ran outside to play tag. I was in so much pain, but terrified to tell anyone. All at once, I opened my mouth to see if the air still hurt. My brother and cousin happened to be running by me. They saw my mouth. They thought I had just fallen. They ran inside and told my parents. Mom was yelling, "How could you do this?"

"It was an accident, Evelyn!" my dad responded.

No one said a word to me in the car going home. I was waiting for the chastisement about how dumb I was. When we all walked into the house, Mom glared at me. She didn't say good night, or ask how badly it hurt, or even try to comfort me through my pain. I went to bed with my mouth aching. I tossed and turned. I couldn't sleep. I finally gave up and lay there as tears ran down the sides of my head.

The next morning, Dad took me to the local dentist. He was a notorious alcoholic. First he told Dad he would put a plastic cap over the tooth with the huge break, but the cap kept cracking and falling off. Then he convinced Dad that both front teeth were dead and needed to be pulled. He said I was making up the pain. He pulled the first tooth out without Novocain. It was excruciating. I was holding on to the arms of the dental chair with all I had. Tears were pouring down my face. I was petrified; his technique was to brace one hand on my head as he rocked the tooth with his dental pliers in the other hand, back and forth until it came out. The pain shot behind my nose, up into my head. I looked at Dad incredulously. Why didn't anyone believe me about how badly it hurt?

I could taste blood, and I thought he was done. Then he told Dad to hold my head still for him so he could pull the other front tooth. His knee came up on the chair to anchor himself. As the tears streamed down my face, I cried out to Dad, "It really hurts!" I could smell booze on the dentist's breath. I knew the smell from the bottles I found in my mom's closet. This time, he did offer to use Novocain. He took a needle and jabbed it into my gum. "She won't feel a thing; I know this one is dead, too." He only waited a couple of seconds and had Dad hold my head again. He braced his knee on the chair harder as he rocked my tooth back and forth. It pinched, and the pain shot back up through my face once again. Tears were running harder now, and I prayed to God to let this be over.

Finally, my tooth gave way and came out. I wanted to scream to the heavens! Why didn't Dad believe me instead of the dentist? I heard the instruments hit the tray. As I looked over, I saw my two teeth and felt so sad for them. I wanted to put them in my pocket, to keep them with me. So I did. I felt such a loss right then. No one saw me.

Dad had business in town and asked if I wanted to stay at the dentist's office to wait for him. I didn't have two front teeth. My mouth was oozing blood. I didn't want anyone to see me. I also was sure as hell not going to stay at that dental office.

The dentist told Dad it would be a couple of weeks before the partial plate would be ready. I was mortified. I didn't want to smile because I felt so ugly.

Normally, a child wants to go home after having a traumatic experience. Not I. I told Dad I needed to check out a book, so I went to the town library across the street and waited there.

I sat at a table and pretended to read. I could taste the blood that seeped down my throat. The gauze wasn't holding the blood anymore, so I just kept swallowing. No one was in there to yell at me; it was quiet. I was learning how to escape from the reality of my world. I told myself to just go somewhere inside my mind and hide. As I pretended to read, I could hear the big clock ticking, and I just wanted to cry. I felt alone and flooded by chills. My body ached. I fought back tears, thinking, *Please! Why can't this stop?*

Summertime came, and we had vacation from school. I played outside, sometimes with my siblings, but mostly by myself. I would get creative with the outdoors, playing in my dad's shop. The building was large enough for a combine plus a couple of tractors. There was a roof, but the floor was all dirt except for one squared-off area where Dad had poured concrete. Right in the middle of the little area, Dad had a large four-foot-tall tree stump he used as a worktable. I pretended that whole area was my playhouse.

I talked to myself constantly, pretending my homelife was what I wanted it to be. I crawled up on the tractors and imagined driving off to different places.

I avoided going inside, even to go to the bathroom. I just peed outside. If I got hungry, I would sneak into the kitchen to make a white bread, mustard, and onion sandwich. Apart from that, I managed to stay outside most of the day.

Many days were spent walking through the shelter of the trees we had behind the house. There, I would listen as the wind blew through the leaves. I would wander over to the feedlot, sit on the feed bunks, and just watch the steers and heifers. They didn't seem bothered by me at all. I loved the pig yard and the piglets, but the smell was such that I couldn't stay long. When the sun cooled on my skin, I knew it was coming time to go back inside the house.

One evening, I had a very hard time swallowing. It had gotten steadily worse over recent months. Dad took me to the doctor, and he said I needed my tonsils out.

"You will fall asleep and not feel a thing," Dad told me as we drove to the hospital. Mom stayed home with my sister and brother. It didn't bug me, but I did notice, as life went on, it was usually Dad who took me to things.

When the surgery was over, they didn't keep me overnight. I lay on Dad's lap as he drove home. The next day, I kept feeling the need to swallow. Mom was washing dishes. I tried to tell her I felt like something was running down my throat. She barely reacted to hearing me. All she said was, "Go lie down."

That evening, Dad was sitting on the couch in his white long johns. I curled up by him and decided not to say anything more about my swallowing.

"What's the matter with you?" Dad asked, looking at me. I said I didn't feel very good.

"She's just being a baby. She's making it up." Mom was standing there, glaring at me. My stomach was getting more and more upset. Mom walked by all dressed up and said she was leaving for her women's meeting. "You just go to bed," she said as she left.

I told Dad my stomach hurt. He was gentle. "Let's watch TV. Maybe you will feel better tomorrow."

I kept swallowing all the time, and it was getting worse. I began feeling dizzy and weak as I lay there thinking, *Don't say anything. It's going to be okay.* All at once, it hit—I had blood coming up into my mouth, and I started gagging. I threw up blood all over Dad's long underwear. I stood up and tried to walk to the bathroom. I threw up a large puddle of blood on the floor. I had trouble standing. Dad grabbed me and sat me on a chair, holding me as I was getting faint. The room started to spin.

I don't remember much after that. I know he must have gotten Mom home for the other kids. Then he was sitting by my hospital bedside. I looked up and saw a bag of blood with a tube running down to my arm. There was pain in my arm.

"You needed some blood, honey," he said. "It's okay." He squeezed my hand. It was just Dad and me again. I was trying hard not to cry. Dad smiled. "You know what, little one? You will be rich someday," he said. I asked Dad why. "Well, they had trouble finding your blood type, and a man that owns part of the bank here in Ord gave you some of his blood." I thought about it for a while and told Dad I would have to write him a thank-you note.

I found out when I got older what had happened. My tonsils were so big the doctor had cut too deeply when he took them out. I was swallowing my own blood until my stomach couldn't take it anymore.

We went home, and I walked in. I looked at Mom. I wanted a hug. "Well, you're home," she said. That was it. I could tell she didn't want to hold me. I just looked away, saw my Coco, and went to bed.

Carol, my friend from school, lived just over the hill from us. She would come over to play, or sometimes, we met on the gravel road with our bikes. We would sneak down and swim in the irrigation ditch. We were clueless to its dangers—its racing, dirty water that rose up to our necks. We weren't thinking about how we could have drowned.

One day, we were messing around, and my plate with my two front teeth slipped out, falling into the muddy water. I knew I was dead if I lost it. I would be belted and reminded of how stupid I was. I wanted to run away. Carol looked at me so funnily. I am sure without front teeth, I looked shocking. "You'd better go tell your mom what happened," Carol said.

I couldn't tell Carol how Mom was. I was ashamed of Mom. I wanted so much to convince Carol to come up to the house with me when I told Mom about losing my fake teeth, but I couldn't. I didn't want Carol to see what would happen. How could I explain that my mom wasn't like her mom? That she would rant about how people were watching us, how stupid Dad was because he wasn't wearing the right colors, and that because of Dad, bad things were happening to the family. I was a target as well, since I continued to hear, "You're just like your dad, so stupid!"

I just couldn't let Carol see this, so with heavy steps, I made my way up to the house, having already prepared myself for the inevitable. It was worse than I imagined. The yelling and cussing, the hard hit to my head. Mom's sharp tongue lashed out at me for days, long enough to get me believing that I really was a dumbbell.

The dentist said he would order me another flipper. It would take a few more weeks to arrive. I would once again have no front teeth. "You are costing us a lot of money!" Mom reached out, yanking my hair, and said, "Are you listening to me? I can't believe you're my kid. You're dumber than a barn door!" Then she quickly switched subjects with no transition at all. "If Dad would just move us from this place, we would be fine."

About three days after I lost my flipper, Carol came over, and we went back to the swimming hole. I told her I wanted to try to find it. We both knew how unrealistic that was, but I prayed, and she said she had been praying, too. By the grace of God, as Carol was walking in the racing, muddy, mucky, water with me, she said, "I'm standing on something sharp."

"Don't move!" I said, and I dove down into the disgusting water, I felt her leg, and pulled myself down to her foot. I couldn't see a thing, so with my eyes closed, I felt under her foot, and there it was—my flipper! I raced to the top of the water and threw my arms around her neck, hugging her so hard. "You found it! You found it!" The flipper had sharp ends, and they had pricked her foot. I couldn't quit telling Carol, "I love you. You saved my life!"

The angels were taking care of me in this moment. There is no other explanation for finding the flipper in those conditions. Someone in heaven had their wings around me. God was watching out for me. I just knew it.

We raced up the hill to tell Mom the good news. I was hoping this would put an end to the yelling and Mom would be happy again. She was pleased, and for a time, life was good.

Mom took me to town the day after I had my teeth back so I could buy Carol a thank-you gift. I loved Mom that day. At that moment, shopping at a variety store with her, I wondered if this was how other girls felt with their moms. Mom let me pick out different things that I thought Carol would like, and we bought a basket to put all the goodies in.

Mom drove me to her home, and I knocked on the front door. Carol had me come in; I thanked her again. I couldn't tell her why my mom never came to the door with me. I'm not sure I knew either, but Mom always had a reason. The reason always made sense to her, but rarely to me. It was all about her paranoia. Maybe the way the cars were parked in their yard. Or maybe it was the color of the front porch rug. I didn't want to ask for fear she would go into a rage and let me have it right there, or worse, say something to my friend. I was glad she didn't want to come in because I was becoming more and more embarrassed by my mom.

When school started up again, I sat by Carol and her sister on the bus. She never knew she was my comfort and joy every morning. My childhood friend. I would remember and carry her with me my whole life, though we never kept in contact.

IT'S LIKE A MOVIE

Grandma Ella would play the piano when she came over. She could play and sing a lot of songs, though "You Are My Sunshine" was her favorite. My mother could play as well. Mom always played "Green Beret." I didn't think either one could sing well, but it made them happy, and that was enough for me. I didn't know my mother was also in anguish; I didn't understand the nuance and complexities of mental illness. I thought in simpler terms. There was the beautiful mother . . . the one who took me shopping for Carol and had held me tightly in her arms on the way to the hospital, and then there was this other being, the one I thought was mean and ugly. It was like there was a giant coin inside her, constantly flipping. The two sides seemed to have almost no relation to each other, and while I knew how to flip the coin from good to bad, I had no idea how to flip it back again. How to bring the beautiful mother back out. I always wanted to tell Grandma what was happening, but I didn't have the strength or guts to do it. Besides, the mean mother never showed her face when Grandma was around.

Mom and Grandma weren't the only family members who played instruments. My great-grandpa and my uncle did, too. Mom decided I should also learn to play the piano.

Mom took me to a house where I would take lessons. It was a huge old white house with thick bushes all around it and paint peeling off its sides. It felt spooky, like a haunted house. Mom walked up to the front door and said she'd introduce me. Then, she would go get groceries and pick me up later. I wanted to scream when the door opened; I knew I was in hell. My teacher looked exactly like the bad witch from *The Wizard of Oz*. The house was dark and smelled of mold. It even felt haunted. The teacher told me to go and sit on the bench in front of the piano. A small lamp shone a thin light on the music book and keys. I could hardly see the notes.

Lessons continued once a week, but I hated them. If I hit a wrong note, she whacked my fingers with the small wooden stick she held for just such occasions. It would send me right to the feelings I had when Mom hit me. I had a rage building in me.

Mom made me practice the piano at home. I really think I would have loved playing the piano, but I was scared of the teacher. I kept trying to practice, and I just couldn't do it. I ran outside and hid in the trees, hoping no one would make me go back to the mean piano teacher. Mom came after me and screamed like I was the devil. The lessons ended, and nothing was said anymore. My grandma let me know her disappointment in me, but Mom never verbalized anything. It was as though it wasn't registering in her.

Something was beginning to occur to me during this time in my life: I was the only one getting yelled at and hit—not my brother or sister. If they did get spanked, it was for something they did wrong. Their spankings never came out of the blue.

I could tell when it was time for me to run upstairs and hide under my big bed. Mom would tell me to come out, and when I wouldn't do it, she'd race off and get the large, green dust mop. I would take as many pokes as I could, just seeing if Mom would stop, and if she didn't, I would crawl out and take my beating.

I started to get smart when I saw Mom winding up, knowing she wanted to hit me. There was a door in my bedroom that went to a dark attic. I hated it, but it always kept me safe. I would sneak upstairs, get in, and close the door. When Mom came up yelling and looking for me, she never thought I was in the attic. She never opened the door. Thankfully, it didn't occur to her that this had become my safe place. She thought I'd made it outside, so she'd go out into the yard and yell for me, receiving no answer.

Sometimes, if it was summertime, I could open my bedroom window. There was no screen on it, and I could climb out onto the roof and sit. I would let the window down behind me, and Mom never figured out where I was.

I can't imagine Mom's chaos—losing her mind while ordinary life happened all around her.

If I had been older, this one time, I would have stood up for my mom even though my feelings toward her were confused. But I didn't.

Labor Day weekend meant our family would spend a couple of days in our small country town. I loved these weekends. It felt so good to run around with other girls, laughing and carrying on, not having to think about Mom all the time. Dad loved to enter a float in the Labor Day parade. This particular year, he had his big red tractor pull a flatbed wagon with a furrowing crate on it. He put a real mother pig inside. He attached stalks of corn and milo to it, and a friend stood holding a spade to represent the American farmer.

There was a lot going on: rides for kids, cotton candy, music . . . It was the typical small-town carnival.

Music was playing on an outdoor stage, and Mom was in a good mood, taking it all in. Dad laughed with his buddies, and we enjoyed the rides and food.

It was getting toward evening, and Dad said it was time to go home. We were all tired and went to bed as soon as we got there.

Soon after the carnival, I heard Mom crying. "See, Richard, someone is shooting at the house when you're not home. There are holes in the side of the house. I will show you. And now they are stealing our chicken fryers." Her words are clear in my memory.

We always ate meals at home. Mom fixed the meat we butchered. Chicken, beef, and pork were all kept in the big freezer on the porch. Dad and Mom had frozen 250 fryers they'd raised from baby chicks. They did this every year, which gave us all the chicken we needed until the next year. They were in our deep freezer, and now they really were gone. Someone *had* stolen our meat.

Mom wasn't in a good place at this time. She was gripped by paranoia, convinced people were still shooting at us, and she was sure they were going to haul Dad away. This event just sent her to the moon, adding to all her fear and anxiety.

Dad and my grandma sat with Mom at the kitchen table. I stood quietly by the oven, somewhat out of sight. I watched my mom's fingers as they kept rubbing the table over and over again.

Dad seemed to keep looking at his coffee cup, and Grandma kept saying, "Evelyn, you're not yourself."

Mom was looking out the window, repeating, "Richard, don't be stupid." The room was quiet. Then Mom's voice got louder. "Why can't you see what they're doing to us?" There was a look of fear in her eyes and anger in her tone. I noticed the look Grandma was giving her daughter, full of shame. I thought Mom must also feel unloved.

She started moving things around; she said objects in our home had to be turned a certain way. She listened to people talking on the party line more and more. Mom thought they were plotting against us and were talking about Dad. It was in code, but she understood it. She couldn't let it go. She kept asking Dad why he was so stupid and why we couldn't move before they killed us all. She said he was being blind to the situation; he wasn't wearing or doing what he was supposed to. She was convinced the FBI and the government were coming for him. How was she going to run the farm and take care of us kids when they locked him up?

Sometime later, Mom was taken away to the mental institution for another stay. Our neighbors were in the kitchen talking with my father. I don't know if they were caught, or how it all came out, but Dad found out they had taken our chickens. They stole them for meat for their family while we were at the carnival. They had once been good friends of my folks, but we didn't see them around after that.

If they hadn't stolen from my family, it might have spared my mother excess mental anguish. I know that even though I was feeling unloved, scared, and nervous, I did feel sorry for her. I was trying so hard to hang on to my own love for her. She would return home and again seem better. The yelling, and trying to convince Dad people were out to get him, stopped. I always thought when she came home things would be different and my relationship with Mom would be good. I always loved that I wasn't being hit or told how much of a mistake I was. Times like these felt like being at an ocean with a warm summer breeze listening to the waves hit the sand. Nothing but peace. I recall going down by the river with the family, playing in the water, and having the most wonderful picnics. Other times, she would even curl my hair and then brush it. I could feel her hands on me in such a gentle touch. It was like medicine for my heart. It was these moments that never lasted long. I could always tell when the fun was about to be over. The stare would come back to her eyes, and with it, my fear of her would return like a knife going into my stomach.

Mom was spiraling deeper into the idea that people were out to get us. It was a Saturday afternoon, and we were all in the car. Dad and Mom had taken us to town to get groceries. I was staring out the window. We were almost home.

We were pulling into the yard when my mother let out a deafening scream. "Oh my God, Richard! Look, they have killed all our little pigs!"

I looked out the car window and saw what looked like bumps of dirt all over the yard.

Mom started screaming again, "I told you they are going to hurt us!" I could see baby pigs in the yard, by the gas barrels on the steps to the house. "They might kill us!" she continued. "Do you think they're in the house?" Dad slammed the car into park, got out, and started running to the mounds of pigs.

I was scared, not sure what to do. I didn't want to get out of the car. "They're here. I just know it!" Mom kept yelling. I opened the car door slowly and went up to one of the little pigs.

I looked all around trying to see if people were here like Mom said. There were so many pigs.

Mom kept yelling, "What is happening?"

Dad yelled back, "Shut up, Evelyn!"

All of a sudden, he heard another little pig squeal loudly from the pen. He started running in that direction. I ran behind him. I stopped, unsure of what I might see. I couldn't get too close to the squealing. I watched my dad pick a couple of the little pigs up that weren't dead yet, and he watched them struggling to breathe. Dad let out a yell I hadn't ever heard. "What the hell has happened!" He kept looking at the pen in disbelief.

I looked back at Mom standing by the house; she seemed out of control. I had no idea where my sister and brother were. I just stood frozen. I saw Dad race by me. I loved all our animals, so I slowly went up to the ones in our fenced-in yard and looked to see if they were still alive. Off to the side by our lilac tree stood my Coco and another little dog we had acquired named Tiger. They wouldn't move, as if they were scared to death. We also had a German shepherd named Rex, but I couldn't see him anywhere.

Once again, I heard a pig squeal. Dad went running toward the pen, where some of the pigs were still alive. That's when we could see Rex chasing a little pig and trying to bite it. I watched, horrified. I couldn't believe Rex was killing all the pigs.

I had never seen my father so mad. He grabbed the dog by the neck. Rex started yelping in pain. I watched Dad grab a chuck of barbwire. He proceeded to drag Rex up to the yard. I don't know how he did it. I couldn't watch because Rex was yelping loudly. I could hear my dad. "You son of a bitch! You want a pig! I'll give you one!"

I felt sorry for Dad. Between the pigs, cattle, and raising crops, he worked hard every day to make our living. All the money lying on the ground must have devastated him. All the work gone just like that. My father loved his animals. He took pride in the farm. The yelping stopped, and I turned to see Rex running around with a piece of barbwire tied around his collar. It had a dead pig hanging from it. As I stood near Dad, he started to talk. "All that money gone! It will be months before the sows can have more babies. We need that money. What am I going to tell the banker?" I looked up at Dad's red face and saw his eyes full of tears. I noticed his hands were shaking. I felt so sad for him. I went and got our little red wagon. I pulled it to each dead little pig and carefully picked them up and put them in the wagon. Dad looked at me and said gently, "When you get your wagon full, go put them on a pile by the furrowing house. I will call the rendering truck to come get them."

I could hear my dad say, "Evelyn, you're talking crazy. It was the damn dog!"

They went inside the house. As the screen door slammed, I looked at Rex. I was sad for him, but I was upset he'd hurt the little pigs. It was a lot to process. I wasn't going to go in the house. I could still hear Dad yelling. I decided to walk around the whole yard and make sure I didn't miss any pigs. I noticed Rex just stayed by the house. He didn't want to follow me.

Later, I sat on our step and looked at Rex, lying there with the dead pig under his neck. *Why did you do it, boy? What were you thinking?* He just looked at me. *You're just as dumb as I am, Rex. You're a goddamn dumbbell.* Some days later, the pig must have rotted and fallen off the barbwire collar. I can't remember, but it seemed a short time after that, Rex was gone, too. No one spoke of him at all.

SHARED A LOVE

One beautiful thing I didn't know then, and only discovered when I was a grown woman, was that my mother loved animals as much as I did. She had pet chickens, raccoons, horses, cats, and dogs. It helps me understand a beautiful part of her that endured even beyond the severe mania and schizophrenia. She let me have all the pets I wanted. I had dogs, horses, raccoons, little coyotes, a skunk, squirrel, calves, cats, and rabbits. Our farm, being outside in nature, was my salvation.

It was an unspoken connection I had with my mother. It was like some part of her knew I needed some love, and I could have that with my animals. I think she knew she was unable to reach inside herself to give that to me. I pictured a brain with a river running through it, and my mother, never knowing day to day where the current would lead and what sandbar she would find. Sometimes, Mom would interact with whatever animal I had at the moment. She'd stroke its coat, and I could see her relax and become calm almost instantly. I wondered what she was thinking, and if she was scared of the imminent next bad spell.

Our yard was full of old tires, sheet metal, and a wide variety of objects just perfect for mice to nest in. Coco would look at me with her big chocolate eyes, pleading for me to help her go hunting. I'd lift a tire as Coco smelled and tracked the mice. I would move with her around the yard, lifting objects and watching her in the thrill of the hunt. The time I spent with Coco made me feel like a normal little girl. I could get lost with her in the daily joys of living on a farm. Coco was the best friend a child could ask for; I relied on her to comfort and listen to me when no one else would.

One afternoon, I went into town with my mom to the grocery store. We returned home near suppertime, which was when I usually let Coco in for the evening. I went all over the yard yelling her name. Normally, she came running. She was never far away from the house. I got worried and told Dad. He yelled for her and looked around. It was starting to get dark, and my parents made me come inside the house. I was crying hard. I wanted to stay outside until I found her. Mom wanted me to eat supper, but I couldn't eat anything, nor could I sleep that night.

I got up the next morning, racing outside to look for my dog. Dad came walking from the direction of the barn and feed house. He looked sad, and I asked him, "Did you find Coco, Dad? Please help me!" Dad sat me down on our front steps and told me that the feed truck delivery guy must have locked Coco inside the shed. I started to get up and said, "Let's get her out!" Dad grabbed my arm and said that Coco must have eaten mice poison, which made her jump through the window. She had died. I screamed loudly, crying, "I have to see her!" Dad took me to the hay pile where she had landed. She was stiff and cold. I petted her head and hugged her body. Dad went to the shop and got a spade, and we buried her behind the shed.

I wanted to yell at the feed man for what he had done. No-body said any more about it, and I carried my sadness within me. This was the first pet I'd lost, and I felt like I was going to die, too. Already in my early life, I knew animals had a spe-cial place in my heart. They were the constant I needed to stay grounded in my environment.

Dad came home one day, and to my surprise, he had bought me a black-and-white Shetland pony. I named her Taffy. She became my new best friend. I got her to climb the three steps separating our farmyard from the private, fenced-in, green grass lawn. I rode Taffy up and over those steps like a bridge, as if the passage transported me into another world, one where I was safe. When we were in the fenced yard, it was like arms were around me. It was a peaceful feeling. There wasn't any shelter that was resilient to the reaches of mental illness. So, as I rode over the steps, I pretended I was going to my safe place. The yard was sizable, and Taffy and I could hide behind big lilac trees.

I could go away to a fantasy of fun. Because it was fenced in, Taffy couldn't run off, not that she ever tried. I could close my eyes, lie down on her back as she walked and grazed on the lawn, and all would be right with the world for those precious moments.

One of my escapes was going into the fields of corn and milo, where I could run between the rows and hide far away from the house. I never knew when the yelling and spanking would start up again, but in the shadows of cornstalks, there was peace. No matter how far out I got, I could hear Mom's voice, yelling at me to come into the house "this instant!" Then I'd hear, "You stupid little shit! Get over here! I'm going to beat the hell out of you! Get in this house right now!" I waited a bit longer, knowing that eventually I would have to return.

The dread of being home with Mom in the afternoons when she snapped suffocated me. I could barely force myself to enter the porch that kept me on edge and held me hostage until I could once again escape to the solace outside.

One day, Mom handed me a bag. "Open it and put it on." It was an outfit that looked like what people wear in a band. "Get it on and get on your Taffy." I kept telling her I didn't want to put it on. I hated it. Then came the hit. "You're ungrateful."

Needless to say, I put it on. I could tell Mom was getting very mad at me. I got on my horse, and she took a picture. I could have died. I hated this picture, and for some reason, I still have it. After the picture, I ran to my room, took the outfit off, and hid it under my bed, hoping to never have to put it on again. Mom kept saying to me as I sat on the horse, "We need to show them you have white on and that you understand what color to wear."

I just stared at her as she took the picture, wondering why she was having me sit on my horse in this majorette costume. None of it made sense to me. I couldn't understand all her crazy words. I tried, but they just made no sense.

One day, when Mom was actually in a good place, she decided to run errands in town. I was happy to stay home and play with Taffy. Mom had no trouble leaving me now that I was older. Maybe it was a relief she didn't have to have me around. Dad was in the fields working. I wanted to watch television, and instead of making Taffy wait outside all by herself where she'd be lonely, I invited her into the house. She wasn't scared; she just followed me in as if she were a large dog. Taffy relaxed and stood in the living room watching TV and napping by me.

When I heard Mom open the door to the house, fear clenched me. All I could do was stand by Taffy and wait. Fortunately, that day, all that came was laughter, followed by tears streaming down Mom's face. I can still see her leaning against the couch, doubled over. The only words she said to me were, "Get Taffy out of the house before you end up having to clean up a mess!" Moments like these were rare and getting further apart, but they remain forever in my heart.

The very next day, Dad found a baby squirrel in a tree he'd knocked down to make room for his new cattle feedlot. I was able to keep the squirrel for a pet. The mother had abandoned it, so I got a toy doll's baby bottle, put milk in it, and put it to his little mouth as I watched him lick it so softly. I had a special way with wild animals. They weren't scared of me, nor was I scared of them.

Throughout my young years, I had many animals. They were therapeutic for my soul, but when one passed, I always felt I died a little, too. The lesson of unconditional love was being taught to me without me even knowing it.

Mom's illness continued to worsen. She began to hit me even more frequently, always accompanying the physical abuse with statements about how dumb I was. She'd taken to pulling my hair and holding me down so I would have to listen to her. These moments were becoming increasingly common. I wished she would do these things to me in front of Dad, but that never happened; he was always working. I started to wonder how my dad dealt with it. Right in front of us kids, Mom would say how stupid he was and that we needed to move. "You have to move us. I can't get better here."

I noticed my father's face becoming more haggard; he had lost the sparkle in his eyes. I was beginning to think this was taking a toll on Dad's faith, and I wondered if he still believed everything would get better one day.

I knew how hard Dad worked on the farm, and I believed he would protect me if he could. But one day, he didn't.

We were butchering chickens. He would cut their heads off with an ax, turn them upside down, and put them into a coffee can nailed to the tree stump so they would bleed out. If the head got cut off but the chicken didn't get into the coffee can right away, it would flap its wings, spurting blood and flopping wildly on the ground. It was horrific to watch.

One chicken got away from me. It started running without its head, its wings flapping too hard for me to catch it, and it ended up under the family car. It had rained hard the night before, and the yard was muddy.

Dad must have been up to his neck dealing with Mom's illness, trying to run the farm, and managing to pay all the bills. He wasn't handling it all well, and that day, he snapped. I had never seen him like that. He told me to crawl under the car to get the chicken. I couldn't do it. I was terrified. Dad grabbed me by the back of the neck and shoved me facedown under the car. My eyes and mouth were packed with mud, and I started crying. I grabbed the chicken's leg, and Dad pulled me back. He took the chicken and went back to the tree stump to kill more chickens, leaving me feeling deserted.

I went in the house. The screen door slammed behind me. Mud was up my nose and in my teeth. I started to rinse my face as tears poured out. I had such an ache inside my chest. Dad was such a loving, kind person. Who was this man who was being so mean? I didn't know him that day.

I ran upstairs to my bedroom and cried ceaselessly. What was happening to the only person I had faith in? He was the only person I could truly trust. I had so much love for my dad, but in that moment, I wondered if I needed to fear him, too. It was overwhelming. I considered whether anyone loved me or if this was my new normal. I had so many questions going through my head; all I could do was cry.

I began to have the thought that it would be better if I were not around. A voice kept repeating over and over in my head, *It would be better if you were dead. It would be better if you were dead.* This thought stopped my tears and left my arms feeling cold.

I finally got the courage to go back outside. I looked over at the old chicken coop, where Dad and Mom were working on the chickens. "Get over here and help!" Dad hollered out. I felt frozen as I sat down on the old folding chair and started to rub and pick feathers from the headless chicken.

Days later, I was chasing cattle in the pasture with Dad. The saddle turned on my horse while I was racing downhill at full speed. As the saddle swung under my horse's belly, her legs pounded the ground around me. I held my head up to keep from banging it against the ground. I thought I would be trampled. My body slammed into the ground, hitting it hard and coming to a stop. I thought that Dad would turn around to help me. I thought if I stayed on the ground and didn't move, I would see how much Dad really loved me. This was my test of his love, but all I got was, "Get your ass up and get on that horse. Cinch that saddle tighter this time!"

I wanted someone to give a damn about me, but that was not going to happen. Instead, it seemed I was losing Dad, too.

It was time once again for my uncle and hired men to round up our cattle and work them: pregnancy-check the cows, vaccinate the calves, and complete all the tasks of the spring cattle cycle. The men were all working at the barn.

I was sitting in my dad's pickup when I saw my uncle's bill-fold on the dash. I looked inside and saw a hundred-dollar bill. For some time, I'd had the feeling Dad was sad. He was increasingly angry and frustrated, and I wanted him to feel better. I knew his birthday was coming up, so I took the hundred dollars and hid it in my room.

In a couple of days, Mom said she needed to go to town. I told her I had saved up some allowance money, and I wanted to buy something for Dad's birthday. Mom never questioned me. I asked her if I could go into the Coast to Coast store to get the present. She dropped me off, saying she would be shopping next door, and to go to the car when I was done. I went in and asked the lady for some tools. I didn't know anything about tools at this point in my life. Somehow, she helped me to get a hammer, some wrenches, pliers, and some screwdrivers—enough to add up to the hundred dollars. The lady put them all in a big bag inside a box. The box was so heavy, I could hardly carry it. The lady helped me by opening the door to the car and putting the box in the back seat.

Dad's birthday came, and I had wrapped each piece separately, so it would look like a lot of presents. As he opened each one, he kept saying, "Thank you," and "Oh my, this sure is a lot of tools," the words softly spoken. I could tell he was surprised. Mom looked at me with disbelief and didn't say anything. Dad looked at Mom like, "I know now that you are behind this gift." I didn't realize it, but he knew I couldn't have bought all this. As I watched him, I wanted him to know how much I loved him and not to be sad or angry anymore.

The next day, I saw my uncle drive into the yard. I was terrified that he knew I had taken his money. I ran up to my bedroom and watched them out of my window. I saw Dad shaking his head and my uncle putting his hand on Dad's shoulder. I didn't know what to do.

I wanted to tell my uncle I was sorry and to tell him why I took the money. He came into the house, and I could hear him visiting with Mom. I couldn't bring myself to go downstairs.

When I saw him leave, I thought I was in terrible trouble, but no one ever said a word to me. I know Dad had to have paid my uncle back, but I don't know why nothing was ever said to me. When I saw my uncle after that, he still gave me the warmest hugs. Maybe he knew more than I thought.

I could tell something was wrong again when my grandma came to stay with us. Almost a year had passed since I'd stolen money from my uncle.

By this time, I had pet geese. I'd raised these geese from goslings and had even saved them from a storm. We had a hailstorm one afternoon, and the hail was as big as golf balls. As I looked out the window to check on my geese, I was shocked. Dad had made a pen around the old doghouse, but for some reason, they weren't going into the old doghouse for shelter. They were just being stupid, standing there getting hit by the hail. I ran outside as fast as I could. The hail was pounding me, stinging my back, head, and arms. I got to the geese and pushed them one by one into the doghouse and shut the door, thanking God they were all okay.

I came home from school one day to find my grandma butchering my geese. What the hell was happening? Everyone knew how I felt about my pets.

My grandma was holding one of my geese by the neck, dead. I screamed out, "What are you doing, Grandma? Stop!

Stop!" She never said a word and went into the house to finish cutting up my geese for the freezer.

Dad told me later on in the day, "You know we butcher our meat to eat. You have seen us butcher chickens, steer for beef, and pigs for pork. Your grandma wants to cook a goose once in a while."

I couldn't say anything, but in my heart, I hated this part of being on a farm.

Everything, even my grandma, had a different look. I knew it was time for Mom to leave again. No one smiled anymore. Mom wanted a picture of us. They took a picture of my siblings and me. There was an unspoken sadness. Our faces showed the whole story.

Mom went away, then came back again; it was the never-ending cycle of our lives. She'd get bad and go away, then come home and be better for a little while until, inevitably, she'd slip back into her old ways.

This time, when Mom came home, I stopped praying thankfully and started asking God questions instead. "Dad and Mom love me, right? Please, God, tell me someone loves me!" I just couldn't figure out what was wrong. No one said anything. Life kept going. Then came Christmas.

Mom went shopping and brought home gifts even though it wasn't Christmas Day yet. She had bought great gifts for my brother and my little sister. I was watching and saying how nice it was to see them get things.

I thought I wasn't getting anything when Mom reached to the very bottom of a large bag and pulled out the strangest gift I had ever seen: a little mouse made of mink fur that could be pinned on a sweater or blouse. It looked like it had diamonds for eyes, but was so realistic, it even had a rubbery tail.

I hated the mouse. I was devastated this was my gift. I said thank you, then left the room and went into the dark kitchen. I crawled under the kitchen table, hurt, and heartbroken. My little brother crawled under the table with me and asked why I was crying, but I wouldn't answer. I told him to leave me alone. He went back out and told them I was crying because I didn't like my gift.

Even though the pin was a mouse and I loved animals, even though it had jeweled eyes, it seemed to me it was really just her way of telling me she thought I was a rat—that I was telling secrets about her to Dad.

Had Dad told her things I'd said? Had she overheard me talking to Dad about people who were supposedly after us? I told him about things that bugged me, about people Mom said were making fun of him. I asked him what things meant when I didn't understand. I wanted to know what different colors meant and why Mom made me change shirts if she didn't like the color. I could tell he didn't want to talk about it. He would just say Mom had a sickness.

The feeling of being alone was growing. I walked back through the living room and saw Dad looking at me. Mom's expression was easy to understand, even though she didn't say a word. It was as though I could read her mind. "That's your gift, for running to your dad." She was smirking as I walked past.

Why was I so hurt? The mouse was cute, yet I went upstairs feeling like I could continue crying. I got my pajamas on and reached into my sock drawer. I pulled out a sock, put my mouse in it, and laid it down beside me to fall asleep.

I was in second grade now. I wanted so much to fit in and have friends. I was shy and scared and sometimes didn't know what to say to other girls. I assumed everything I said would be wrong. I had, after all, been told every day just how stupid I was. And so, I did the unthinkable. I lied to a girl at school.

I was riding the bus home, and I wanted to play and have a friend so badly. I told this girl my mom said I could go over to her house to play for a while after school. I vividly remember not wanting to go home. I wanted to escape the reality of what awaited me when I got off the bus. The girl I lied to lived four miles away and always got dropped off last. She agreed to let me come over, and we told the bus driver to drop me off at her house. We played outside with her cats for a while. Then we went inside. Their house looked like mine. We made peanut butter sandwiches. Then we went to her bedroom to play with the cutest dolls I had ever seen. Time seemed to go by slowly. I was savoring this moment.

When her mom came home and found me there, she called my mom. I knew I would be in trouble, but just for a while, I got to experience someone else's normal, to see what other families were like.

I was beaten for it, and this one time, I felt I deserved the beating. Mom had a wooden stick, and she made me run in front of the car. Every time I slowed down, she would get out and hit me hard. I don't know how many miles we went on this way—I suspect about two, before she let me back in the car and drove us the rest of the way home. While the neighbor girl was still nice to me in school, we were never good friends after that. I am sure her family talked about it and thought I was a bad kid for lying. If they only knew the truth. As a child, I wished I could say, "Something is wrong at home with Mom," but I had no idea how to deal with this problem. I believed this was just how my home was and how it would always be. My mom was just different.

I had also changed. I had withdrawn, becoming scared, empty, shy, and nervous. And I created a mental shell around me to cover me and protect me. I never said a word to anyone about the constant tenseness in which I lived.

To get the attention I needed, I lied, saying whatever I thought people wanted to hear. Telling a lie to get a reaction of any kind was okay in my mind. I acted out in peculiar ways. While staying with my aunt, for example, I shoplifted from a variety store. I didn't even know, at the time, why I took the candy—we always had plenty of it in the house. But my aunt disciplined me in a way that made me want to be a better person. She never told my folks; she just took my purse away.

THE ASYLUM

nce again, Mom was gone. This time, I was told she was at Hastings Regional Center. That name would come to burn its brand in my brain forever; Mom would stay there many times.

My first visit to this hospital was somewhat unsettling. The place looked like an old school. We went into the lobby, and Dad told me I'd have to wait there for him to bring Mom out to see me. I didn't know what an institution was yet. No one had ever explained such things to me.

I looked for books to read, but none of the books had stories to which I could relate. I thought I would find a book that described our family, including my mom.

The place stank like a foul-smelling bathroom. I was sitting on a hard, plastic chair when an old man came up to me. He looked like my bus driver. He asked if I was there to help him and his deputies. I didn't respond, because I didn't understand. Then he took out a toy sheriff's badge and pinned it on my shirt. I was quiet; I didn't know what to say. "We are tracking the bad guys who are trying to hurt all of us," he told me. A surge of calm came over me. This old man talked like Mom. I realized there were other people here like my mom. I started to talk to the man. I told him I would wear his badge and be his helper. In the back of my mind, I already knew to cooperate to keep from getting hit or being told I was stupid.

When my dad came into the lobby with Mom, I thought something was wrong with her pants; her clothes didn't look right. It seemed that there was a large bulge on the side of her stomach. Her loose shirt went over it, and the bulge was only on one side. I stood up thinking I would get a hug. That, as always, turned out to be wishful thinking. Dad asked me about my badge, and I said the sheriff gave it to me. Neither Mom nor Dad responded.

We were allowed to take Mom out for a couple of hours, so we went to a nearby mall for lunch and shopping. Time went so fast. I hated hearing Dad say it was time to get Mom back. I was enjoying the mall, looking at all the stores and watching other people shopping. I fantasized about having a fun-loving mother. At the hospital, she seemed calm. I hoped this time she'd be cured, that she'd get better and the paranoia would stop. Bad Mom. Sick Mom. Good Mom. I was tired of not knowing which one I'd get.

When animals on our farm would get sick, I could see the sadness in their eyes. I think I saw that in Mom's eyes this time, and it made me feel sorry for her. In some ways, I could glimpse how much she was suffering, too.

I listened as my mom told Dad how she was better and wanted to go home. Tears filled her eyes. She didn't want to be sick. She wanted to be well. He told her it would be just a bit longer. I didn't understand why Mom couldn't make her own decision about when to come home. She was, after all, a grown-up.

At the same time, a voice inside my head reminded me I was happy when Mom wasn't home. I felt conflicted. I jumped back and forth between wanting a mother, and remembering the mother I had.

I wanted her to be well, to be better, but I also knew maybe . . . just maybe . . . that would never happen. Maybe she'd always be sick. Paranoid. Mean. I was starting to watch other girls at school with their mothers, and I found myself wanting that so badly. Sometimes when I played by myself, I imagined a pretend mom. She was wonderful.

As this visit continued, Dad asked Mom what she had in her pants. I knew something looked funny and thought we should buy her new pants since these didn't fit her right. She reached down and pulled out scores of recipes on three-by-five-inch cards. "Richard, someone is stealing all my things from my room, so I have to hide everything in my pants."

My mind was racing. *Why would they take Mom's things? We need to take Mom home.*

"Maybe the sheriff can help." My suggestion came out of the blue. Dad looked at me with a look like I'd never seen from him, as if he wanted to tell me something but couldn't.

I thought about what I'd overheard Dad telling my uncle. He'd said Mom has delusions, a symptom of schizophrenia, that she believes someone or some people are out to get us and that she believes every event has a personal meaning directed at her.

That explained so many of the things I thought were crazy: the neighbors being out to get us, Dad being in on it, our need to wear certain colors for different reasons. He told my uncle her schizophrenia made her feel unmotivated, so she didn't care about daily activities. He explained why she lost some memories of her past—it was the side effect of her electric shock treatments. The only word that stuck with me was *schizophrenia*.

It was time to say good-bye. We told her we'd see her next weekend. Mom had heavy tears in her eyes. Her mouth quivered. I reached out and squeezed her hand. Mom said, "I really just want to go home." Dad gave her a kiss and a hug and said it wouldn't be long now; she was almost better. I couldn't make sense of Mom being in an institution, because I was unable to see where she was hurt. I wasn't even sure what they did there. I didn't see any doctors, just a woman behind glass doors sitting at a desk. I hoped Mom would get better, so I wouldn't have to see the man with the badge again.

Sometimes Mom would be in the institution for four to five months at a time. These stays were a relief from the abuse, and yet, my heart hurt. The feeling of emptiness was so strong at home. Nothing was being said. The house was just quiet.

When we sat down to eat, the table seemed empty. My dad would turn and look out the window, and his eyes would seem lost in thought. I could tell he missed her. I found myself thinking about the "good" months that followed each institution stay. I let my mind wander through memories, and forget about the bad days.

The best times were when the JCPenney and Sears catalogs arrived in the mail. Mom would let me pick out dresses, tops, and shoes for the next school year. She loved everything I loved. I discovered she loved clothes as much as I did. Other times, I would sit at a table with her and we would lick green stamps and put them in a green stamp book. She would drive us to town, and we could go into the green stamp store. They had everything you could think of for sale, and instead of dollar tags, every item had a ticket that showed how many books of green stamps it would take to purchase it. Mom would use her stamps to get things she needed for the house. When times were good, she would teach me all the recipes she could think of. Then, in the span of a single breath, that would vanish, and things would be back to normal once again.

At home, I was growing up before my time. I learned how to do laundry from Grandma Ella. I started cooking and taking care of my siblings as best I could.

My grandma stayed with us during Mom's breakdowns until my early teenage years. Then we handled things on our own. My uncle and aunt would come over and help when needed. That was our life. It was strange to be running the house with one parent gone. I knew when she returned, there'd be a honeymoon period. How long it would last was anyone's guess. As much as I hoped she'd be cured and would be forever well, I also expected her to backslide. She came home seeming better, but then the slow descent into madness would begin.

First there'd be cursing and some frustration, the odd comment here or there about how stupid Dad was. The irrational moments she'd snap at me. Then, slowly, paranoia would creep back in. She'd talk about the neighbors watching us or about some person at the store wearing a certain color, a signal only she understood. When that happened, it wouldn't be long until she was gone again.

Taking care of the house became therapy for me. I was always trying to please my dad as well. The harder I worked, the better I felt. It was my duty. The weekends came and went, and sometimes my aunt, who was the wife of my mom's brother, would come with us to see Mom. I didn't know why, but I noticed a hurt look in my mom's eyes when my aunt was with us.

I would come to know that Mom was worried she would take Dad away from her. She was jealous in a crazy way. But the threat was real to her, and her pain was deep.

I looked out the back window of the car as we drove away. Mom was standing on the sidewalk, crying hard, watching us go. I silently cried, too. As the tears ran down my face, I noticed no one said a word. We rode home in silence. My tears kept running down my face like a stream from a faucet. I didn't cry easily anymore, but this time, the feelings consumed me. I couldn't stop. Everything I'd packed away wanted to come out. I kept my face pointed toward the window and watched every telephone pole and all the trees go by. I didn't have thoughts running through my head—all I had were tears.

Women frequently asked Dad if he needed help. He always smiled, looked at me, and said, "Nope, my daughter is doing a great job. We are fine." What my father didn't know, and I never shared with anyone, was that I was getting protective of him, our home, and my siblings. No one was going to take anyone else away from us.

Sometimes, when I was scrubbing the floors, I would picture my mom and those tears, and I would clean harder to keep everything right. I may not have liked how Mom was toward me, but to see her cry broke me. I decided to be the rock of the house. I sat and thought of my mother. I wondered how she was feeling, in a strange room with a strange bed, away from her home and family. I wondered how it felt getting better for such a short time and then returning to the confused way of thinking. I started to feel empathy for Mom. I took some deep breaths and got back to work. When Mom was home, every Saturday was "clean-house-spotless day." It was branded into my soul, but now it had a different meaning.

Dad never left us alone when Mom was in the institution. We would watch TV, play cards, or spend time together outside. He was a wonderful father. He made home a safe place for us.

Yet when Mom was away, not a word was ever spoken about her. I didn't understand the silence. I can only tell you what it was like: we acted as though everything was fine. Sometimes I would look at my brother and sister and wonder what was going through their minds. I wondered whether Dad ever went somewhere by himself to cry.

Dad worked constantly outside, and Mom was always in the house. I looked for things to do. One afternoon, I was playing by the huge gas barrels Dad had for all the machinery.

Not knowing any better, I decided to smell the nozzle of the gas hose. Immediately, I was dizzy and couldn't walk straight. I smelled it again and liked that it made me feel goofy. I waited in our yard for a long time, thinking, *I have to go in the house. It's almost suppertime.*

Mom appeared at the screen door. "You'd better get in and wash up. It's time to eat."

I held my breath as I walked past her, hoping she wouldn't notice the scent. She grabbed me by the shoulders. "You goddamn dumbbell! You've been smelling gas!" I was still dizzy from the fumes. I knew I was getting hit hard and fast, but I couldn't feel it at all. My body was hitting against the door. I struggled to keep standing.

Mom sat me down on a chair. As I watched her move around the room, I thought I'd better not do that again, but the truth is, I did love that for a moment, I didn't feel anything. When the numbing sensation wore off, the ache from her blows set in. I started to get a headache from the gas fumes as I waited for Dad to come in for supper. I still wasn't entirely in my head. I could hear the echo of Mom telling my father how stupid I'd been. I couldn't think about anything, though. I just felt numb.

My siblings began spending more time outside, too. We would climb up wooden planks in the barn and get on the back of our big horse, Boots. Then we could grab the top of the barn door and slide off his back as he raced out the doorway of the barn. It was dangerous, but we didn't care. We were always inventing things to do. I wondered whether they were trying to avoid being in the house with Mom, too. I knew she wasn't hitting them as she did me. I never heard her call them *dumbbells*. Still, I think in some ways, it frightened them to be in the house with Mom. I suspect they thought she might start treating them the way she treated me.

One of my chores was to help Dad feed the mother pigs. I never minded this job. Each mama pig received a can of feed and water. They were all in separate crates, each one with their babies in the furrowing barn.

I couldn't lift the awkward five-gallon bucket, so Dad filled a big tub with their feed and gave me a coffee can. Every evening, I went back and forth with the can until I had all of them fed.

The smell was disgusting, but I loved watching the little pigs. Dad would turn on the big radio he had on a shelf. Most of the time, he played polkas, and the little pigs would wiggle their tails to the music.

Sometimes after feeding them, I just sat on an old sack of feed and watched the baby pigs, trying to kill time so I didn't have to go into the house. I was sad and felt like crying, but tears wouldn't come.

Mom's behavior toward me had gotten even worse. I didn't hold a fork right; I didn't shut a random door; there was always a reason, and the beatings came without warning. Sometimes she would chase me, catch me, and beat me hard on my back. I knew, after a while, to just let her hit me to get it over with. I had trained myself not to feel the pain.

One day, I was standing in the middle of our farmyard, and Mom was hitting my back hard with a large stick. My aunt and uncle drove into the yard.

"Evelyn, what are you doing to her?" my uncle said, jumping out of the car. Mom looked at her brother but didn't say a word. Later, my aunt took me aside and asked me why I wasn't crying. I told her I could make my body not feel pain. I saw her puzzled expression, but I couldn't explain it further. I told her not to worry, because it didn't hurt. I would be okay.

I was getting older. Mom would return home after another institution stay, and she treated me as if I didn't exist anymore. When she came into the house, I thought I would have the nice Mom for a while, and things would be good. Instead, she walked right by me as though I wasn't standing there. I had cleaned the house and put a roast in the oven for supper so she didn't have to cook. I went to her and said, "Mom, I have supper in the oven for you." She did not reply. I ran outside as fast as I could. The hurt was overwhelming.

I would have rather been hit or yelled at than ignored. I thought, *What have I done now? Why do you hate me?* I was almost thirteen and felt like an empty body wanting to be loved.

In that setting, a sense of worthlessness became part of my personality. I didn't know it; I just became it.

CHILDHOOD ENDS

One evening, a couple came over, and Dad introduced us to them. This was our new hired man and his wife. All we knew was that he would be working on the place with Dad every day. He had a son who was five years older than I was. Dad hired the son to milk our cow in the evenings.

I was beginning to show signs of puberty. I developed quicker than other girls in my class. I was already starting to fill out. Mom had even noticed and bought me training bras. The hired man's son seemed to notice me, too. He would always wave at me as he drove through the yard. I thought he was cute. I wanted attention more than I even realized.

I started going to the barn when he was milking the cow. He would flirt with me, saying I was growing up and that I was a cutie. This became an everyday fix for me, waiting and watching out my bedroom window for his car to come driving in. The way he would talk to me was intriguing, and though I felt uneasy—good, naughty, nervous—hearing kind words spoken to me was having a powerful effect.

I missed out on the "I love you," other kids had. Our house didn't offer hugs or physical kindness. It's strange what the mind will do to substitute for lost love. My animals had always been the surrogate I turned to, up until now.

I didn't realize I was starving for affection and was vulnerable to do almost anything as long as I felt wanted. I became addicted to those few minutes in the barn each day.

One night, my folks asked him to babysit all of us kids. I was excited, thinking I would hear his intoxicating words again.

His game was hide-and-seek. He told my sister to hide and my brother to count to one hundred. Then he grabbed my hand and pulled me up the stairs to hide. As he looked around my bedroom, he pulled the dresser out from the wall and pulled me behind it with him. We were in darkness as he pulled the dresser back to the wall. We were pinned tightly together, and I could see his hand reaching down inside his jeans. The shadow of the dresser made it hard to see clearly. I felt his tight grip around my hand as he pulled it inside his jeans and whispered to me to touch it. I was petrified. I kept pulling my hand back as hard as I could as he tightened his hold. "I will tell your folks about the times you come to the barn," he whispered sternly.

All of a sudden, I was afraid of losing the boy who had made me feel wanted. Still, I resisted. "I don't want to," I said, my voice shaky. He proceeded to grab my hand and put it on his penis. He held his hand tightly over mine and made my hand go back and forth. He kept saying, "Hold it tighter." I wanted to scream. It felt like holding a stick. Then the words kept coming. "Don't stop or I will tell your mom and dad on you."

Tears filled my eyes, and I couldn't understand what was happening. My arm became rigid and my hand was hurting. I looked at the space between the dresser and the wall, thinking, *How can I get out of here and escape?* I couldn't look at my hand and see what was happening, I kept looking for a space to run. I started to shake hard, and I asked, "Please, let me go. I want you to stop it."

All of a sudden, I heard my brother coming up the stairs looking for us. I was so grateful! I felt him let go of my hand. I pushed the dresser hard. I couldn't run fast enough toward my brother's voice. I wouldn't leave my brother's or sister's side the rest of the night. I sat by them and watched TV, looking at my hand and the red marks all over it. I was scared about what had happened. I didn't know what to think. When my folks returned home, the boy gave me a look. I knew it meant, "Shut up and keep our secret." His smirk unnerved me.

Later when I went to bed, I had a terrible time parsing out the mixed feelings I had inside.

I found myself still craving attention, so I returned to the barn—just for the flirting—the very next afternoon. His attention was more important to me than the head games. I needed to feel wanted. I didn't think I was humiliating myself for a few dirty words of flirting. I just knew I was being noticed—that in some way, to someone, I mattered. That was just what I needed. I wondered if sexuality would be the only way I would find to feel wanted.

I started to worry about how far I would have to go to get attention. Mental abuse was driving me straight toward sexual abuse.

Eventually, the boy got busy with school and quit coming over. Maybe my dad was picking up on things and made it stop. I have no idea. I was relieved, but also found myself missing the attention and compliments, even if they weren't actually nice.

All the while, Mom was drinking more and more. Mom was in her world, and I was lost in mine.

DAD'S ACCIDENT

I f angels can watch over you, they did for our family. It might have been in a rough way, and it was almost at the cost of my father's life, but it gave all of us a moment in time to breathe.

I was in seventh grade. I sat in the back of the schoolroom, listening to the teacher, when there was a knock on the door. It was the principal. We all looked up, and he whispered something to the teacher.

"Karen, you need to get your books and go with the principal."

I was terrified! I had never been called out of a classroom. *What did I do? Who is mad at me? Was Mom downstairs and upset at something I did?* I was afraid Mom was in the office, and whatever it was, they would listen to her. I was sure I was in trouble for something, but I didn't have a clue what it could be.

The principal walked with me and said nothing. We got to the office, and my uncle was there.

"Karen, you have to come with me; your dad has been hurt."

The shock of his words made me feel like my heart had stopped. I couldn't breathe. Was my dad going to be taken away from us?

On a farm, silage is cut and chopped to feed and fatten up the cattle so they can be sold in the fall for meat. September is often chilly in the mornings and hot in the afternoons.

My dad was out cutting silage on an old Farmall H tractor. It had no cab, and the steering wheel and seat were both made of iron. There was a spinning blade below his seat that connected the tractor to the chopper. He was starting to get warm. As the tractor was running, he went to pull off his overalls. One of the sleeves fell down onto the power takeoff (the shaft that rotates at a high speed). It grabbed the sleeve and started pulling him down. He bent the steering wheel almost in half trying not to get pulled onto the spinning shaft. I think of the adrenaline it took to bend iron as the auger kept tugging on him, ripping the clothes off him. The power takeoff drill continued turning and sat my father's butt right on the blades, which ended up penetrating my dad's now-naked body. The blade went up inside his rectum, missing an artery by barely a quarter of an inch.

A neighbor lady who was driving past saw what was happening. Dad was bleeding profusely. She wrapped him in a blanket from her car and took off for the hospital. It was over thirty miles away. She knew when you live out in the country and have a serious accident, chances of survival are slim. It was better to just go. A neighbor man ran to tell Mom, and they all raced to the hospital.

My uncle drove my siblings and me to the hospital in Sargent. The lobby was small, and we looked like three silent rabbits waiting for someone to tell us about our dad.

I heard the doctor tell Mom and my uncle that he would try to put a plastic tube in Dad to act as part of his colon, which the shaft had badly cut. Hours crawled by. Our uncle took us home. Mom stayed with Dad—the love of her life.

The next day, we all got to see him, and Mom told my uncle that Dad was screaming so loudly the whole hospital heard him. He had been bracing so tightly from the pain that he bent the bed rail. Mom was crying, "Richard went back into surgery during the night for over seven hours." All we could do was sit there until the doctor came and told us we could see him. The doctor came toward Mom and said he had to remove the plastic tube. The doctor told Mom surgery took hours because he repaired Dad so he wouldn't need a colon bag attached to his side.

Dr. Westbrook was a saint and a godsend to us all. He was in a small town, but he was a brilliant surgeon. Dad and Mom were eternally grateful.

This was our breathing moment. It seemed as though Mom wasn't sick at all. She took care of my father, who came home and had to spend months in a hospital bed in our living room.

Mom seemed healthy, wrapping herself up in taking care of Dad. She had to put iodine inside my dad's wound for months. He had developed a staph infection while in the hospital. It was a long healing process.

My siblings and I were in school now, and we would come home to see Dad cooking in the kitchen and making caramel apples. It was quiet and calm in our house, the two of them chatting charmingly.

Thank goodness for neighbors and hired help. They took care of our farm and the livestock until Dad could return to his chores.

I could see in Mom's eyes the love she had for Dad. She was so happy he was alive. During this time, there was no yelling, no craziness. There was almost a warmth, even toward me. It was a wonderful moment in time, a period when I could glimpse what life would be like if our mom were well, if she were whole and healthy. I watched my mom watch my dad. I witnessed true love. I hoped, prayed, and talked to my animals. I wanted Mom to be all better now; I wanted scary Mom to be gone forever.

Time moved on, and Mom got worse again. She kept telling my dad to move her to Burwell, where she was from. It wasn't far, just forty minutes away.

"You have to move me where I was raised, where my mother and brother live. I will get better if I live near family." Dad loved Mom so much, he would do anything for her. Maybe something would change, and she would get better. Mom was convinced now that her only hope of getting well was to move.

I could hear her talking to herself in the kitchen, saying how they were going to burn our house to the ground. A strange pickup was in the yard, so I went outside to see who it was. Dad was talking with a gentleman wearing a large gray cowboy hat. I heard him say, "We will get you a good price for your farm. Don't you worry about that. And by the way, I have a farm with a nice house right near Burwell. Let's make an offer."

He had to sell our pasture and buy a new one near Burwell for our cattle. It was a huge change. He had worked his whole young life to build up our farm. He had built huge hog buildings, a large feedlot, and had added on to our home. He was willing to let it all go if it would save my mother, his best friend.

This was another vision of true love's fight against mental illness.

It was summertime, and Dad kept our farm going even as he went to Burwell to get the new farm ready for the cattle, pigs, and chickens. Mom went with him to work on the new house. They were so busy the exhaustion began to show on their faces.

I didn't want to move. I was thirteen and just starting to make a few friends on my own. I would lose them, including

Carol. I spent a lot of time in my bedroom thinking about how different things were going to be. I was scared to switch schools, but my biggest worry was Mom. Would she be okay? Would this actually cure her?

I went with her sometimes to work on the house and discovered her sneaking beer along. My mind was full of secrets. Mom would tell me in the car driving back and forth how much she loved the move. I had become quiet, not even realizing it. Leaving this house was leaving my safe place and all my secret hiding spots.

At the new house, I had to share a bedroom with my sister. It really didn't bug me; I was just aware of the change. Dad made a bedroom downstairs in the basement for my brother. Dad was starting over and needed to rent land again. He also had to buy a big pasture. We were doing the same thing, but in a different place, and it seemed like Dad was having to work even harder. He had to build new pens for the hogs and make a new feedlot for the cattle.

His work was nice, but it wasn't the same. We didn't have big buildings like we'd had before. I never said anything, but I wondered if my dad ever missed our old home.

Mom was so busy unpacking, and Dad was going nonstop outside getting our new farm up to speed. No one said much. I just helped with whatever anyone needed. Summer flew by. It seemed like the move was good for our mother. I couldn't really tell, but she wasn't yelling or talking nonsensically, and I wasn't getting hit. It seemed maybe all was right with the world.

Living in the county, we had to attend a country school until ninth grade. Then we could go to a town school. I had left a school where we were already changing rooms and teachers for each subject, but I was only in eighth grade, so in this area, I was headed to a one-room schoolhouse with kindergarten through eighth grade. I was now in the same room with my sister and brother.

I liked wearing dresses; all the girls at my old school did. I looked around and saw my one and only classmate. She was wearing jeans and a T-shirt. She chewed tobacco. I was stunned; I hated the whole idea of the country school.

I went to the bathroom, and when I returned to my desk, my new classmate had put her newly sharpened pencil straight up on my chair. I sat down right on the sharpened end. It hurt so badly I couldn't scream or even take a breath! My teeth gripped tightly together, and I felt my neck pull straight up. I wanted to slap the hell out of her. She leaned over and said, "You'd better start wearing jeans out here."

I realized that in order for her to like me or even tolerate me, Mom would have to let me wear jeans. I went home and begged Mom to buy me some new western jeans. I told her no one wore dresses because at recess we played outside. I couldn't bring myself to tell her about the pencil incident. I didn't want to risk her going to the school and saying something that would embarrass me. Mom looked at me and said, "Okay. Let's go to town and get your jeans." Thankfully, I wasn't drilled on the matter.

I had a learner's permit, and I was driving my brother and sister to school. This had some humor to it; my brother would get mad when the gravel roads were muddy because I sometimes flirted with the roadside ditch, sliding back and forth, almost getting stuck. I am sure I scared the shit out of them. I always subjected them to my eight-track playing rock and roll music: BTO, Foghat, T. Rex, and Three Dog Night.

We had to bring our own lunches to school. At first, Mom was fixing good sandwiches and all seemed well, but I noticed Mom was always sleeping when we got home from school. I saw beer bottles in the trash. Mom tried to hide them, but I found them anyway. She was changing fast. We had only lived in our new home for four months, and things took a new turn. It was like she couldn't get enough sleep. She would wake up in the morning, fix us breakfast, and head straight to the couch to lie down.

The first big change came without warning. We opened our lunch pails and found nothing but jars of baby food. I had a jar of peas and a jar of applesauce. I watched my brother's eyes. He tried to hide it and ate only a little. It bothered me so much that I had to quit looking at him. My sister looked so confused. I would not eat mine. I was so embarrassed for myself and my siblings. I would sneak my lunch pail into the bathroom and throw the jars into the trash so Mom would think I ate them. Sometimes I couldn't get them into the trash, and she would find them when I got home. She'd yell at me, and I would get the same jars the next day. I wanted to yell back at her, to tell her to quit being crazy, to stop hurting us. I wanted to scream out loud, "You are embarrassing us to death. Stop! Stop already! No more baby food, please!" I was sure the other kids in the room noticed. This continued my whole eighth-grade year.

Finding out that I had fallen behind my peers in schoolwork was devastating. Though my mother had been a brilliant teacher, at home, I got nothing in the form of help with schoolwork.

I started to believe Mom was right about me being dumb. I was struggling in school, and my surroundings made it difficult to concentrate on schoolwork.

I had a wonderful teacher who picked up on the fact that I had been having trouble for a long time. She got permission from my folks to keep me after school, and she worked with me to try to get me caught up. I know she helped me, but I don't know to what level. I was grateful to her, though my grades only came up to average. Still, I was better off than before.

Through the school year, I made friends with my only class-mate. She was a tough person, but she was so much fun. We connected, and she would invite me to stay over at her house. I really learned a lot when I stayed there. It wasn't like our home at all, but I couldn't tell my friend that; I couldn't tell my friend about Mom.

I grew more and more ashamed of my mother. When I was with my friend and her family, I tried to slip away—into a world without my mom and all the emotions that went with being around her. I would do and be whoever my friend wanted me to be. If she did chores, I would help. My friend seemed so grown-up and independent. At her home, they treated her like she was already an adult. We could drink beer. I mentioned I'd like to get my ears pierced. The next thing I knew, she was piercing my ears with a sewing needle and an ice cube. I couldn't believe it. I was thrilled! Then, all of a sudden, I realized I couldn't go home. What would my mom do to me?

The fear was so heavy I had trouble breathing. I knew if I didn't go home, I would be in serious trouble, so I thought I would just wear the earrings, hoping Mom wouldn't notice. Almost the minute I walked into the house, Mom said, "What is that on your ears?"

As soon as the words left her mouth, I knew Mom was start-ing to get bad again. I wondered how long it would be before she would want to hit me or call me names. To my surprise, she said, "Well, they look okay." That statement gave me hope; maybe Mom was going to be okay. Maybe I'd overreacted. Who was being paranoid now?

Soon, I'd find out my first instincts were right. Later that evening, Mom's glare returned. Then the foul words: "I don't know why you want to bring attention to your Mickey Mouse ears." I'd never thought about my ears, and afterward, that was all I could think about. Were they ugly ears? She kept on repeating how tiny my ears were and that they didn't match my head. I found myself looking at my ears all the time. I decided right then the short hair had to go. I needed to grow my hair long enough to cover my little ears.

After neighbors found out we had moved in (and that I was of babysitting age), I started to get some jobs. Dad insisted we know how to work and how to save our money. I always found jobs in the summertime. My favorite job was at the local veterinary clinic. There I got to work with all kinds of animals.

One summer, I got a job at Bo's Dairy Mart. My girlfriend's mom and dad owned it. She worked there as well, so we could see each other at work. I was careful not to complain or to show my discomfort at work, but I had grown to become scared of people. The situation at home had left me with no self-confidence at all. When I walked up to people to wait on them, my insides would tighten like a hard rubber ball. I was so relieved when my work shift was over.

I helped with the hogs, cattle, and chicken chores. My siblings and I helped Dad with anything he needed: moving irrigation pipe, cutting musk thistles in our pastures, or working in the hayfield. This part of our lives felt normal. I assumed every kid did chores. Dad needed our help, and we had fun working with our father. Learning to drive the pickup and tractors was a hoot.

Dad bought himself a brand-new Ford pickup, and I put the first two dents in it. I know it had to hurt him to see the new truck dinged, but he never hit me or yelled at me. He just welded some metal on top of the original end gate so that when I backed up to the chute and bumped it, I wouldn't leave a dent. He looked at our accidents as part of the learning curve. When we moved, he didn't have hired help; his kids were capable of helping with all the chores now. After working outside, we would go into the house, and Mom would have supper ready. When we finished eating, my sister and I took turns doing the dishes. My brother would go downstairs to his room. The house seemed quiet. No laughter. Not much of anything.

Mom was getting sick again. However, this time it was different. Dad had taken her to a new doctor, who put her on a lot of different drugs. There were over seven different bottles in the medicine cabinet that she was to take daily. For some reason, she fixated on wanting us to brush her hair. She couldn't get enough. My arm got so tired, and she would still want me to keep brushing. I made my little sister help me. Mom was getting weird about her body, too. She would scratch herself constantly. It was embarrassing to all of us, and once in a while, Dad would say, "Evelyn, stop already." I kept thinking, *Mom said if we moved she would get well.*

Things were changing in our home, but no one talked about it. We just brushed Mom's hair and pinched pimples on her back whenever she wanted.

I really didn't know how to feel. I went with Mom to the grocery store. We would be pushing our cart down the aisle, when someone would come toward us and all of a sudden turn their cart and head to another aisle to avoid us. A shudder would go through me. I was embarrassed and sorry for my mom. *Why are people treating her funny?* Sometimes, Mom would leave the grocery cart full of groceries, push it so it was pointed a certain way, and make us leave the store and not pay for any of it. I wondered how people knew about Mom. I never said anything. It was so weird. Did they know about her thoughts? Were they aware that things had to be pointed in a certain direction? Did they know about the colors and what they stood for? I had no idea. I didn't know how small-town news got around or that it might have been worse because this was the town where she'd grown up. I figured people must have kept up with what was happening to her. Maybe it was just town gossip. Who knows, but they seemed scared to talk to her. They would avoid Mom like the plague.

We usually picked up Grandma, so she could shop for her groceries as well. I noticed that Mom wasn't doing that any-more. We would drive right by Grandma's house and never stop. Who was helping Grandma get her groceries? She didn't drive. I couldn't bring myself to ask why we stopped going to get her.

Small-town word gets out. People react and talk behind the person's back.

Mom was becoming a stranger in our home. She wanted to go to town functions. Mom wanted to join a church group, the Women's Christian Hour. For some reason, Mom always made me go with her. In this new group, with Mom saying the things she did, I never knew whether the women were sitting away from Mom or whether Mom was sitting away from them. Mom just sat there and stared off into space. She did not participate in their conversations. Sometimes, she would let out an unprovoked laugh and say something that had no meaning whatsoever. The women would look down and not say anything. It was dead silent.

Some of the women stared at Mom, and I could tell they were talking about her. I wished I had been older and could have given them a sermon. I wanted my mom to quit going.

She really was getting deranged thoughts about where people sat, the colors they had on, the kind of cars they drove, the position of anything . . . Their purses had to point a certain way. They should be sitting with their hands folded a certain way, or their book on the table should be opened to a certain page. I sat quietly and did not say a word to anyone. They never said a word to me, either. I thought maybe, just like me, they were too scared to say anything. I was growing more and more embarrassed of my mother.

THE CHANGE

This nervous breakdown was difficult to watch. Mom had been acting weird for about a year now, but we were all just learning to live with it and not have her shipped off to an institution again. I think Dad was tired of paying for it. She would come home, and the sickness would raise its ugly head again. None of us liked it, but we tolerated the situation as best we could.

One day, Mom took me to town and said we were going to the Westside Tavern. We sat down at a table. Mom was observing people. "They think I don't know what color to put on when I drive east down the road." Her words came spooling out. My mother's laugh overtook the room. I hated being in there with her. I wanted to run out. The lady behind the bar just looked at us. "They think I don't know what it means when they drive by me in a red car, but I know what that means." I watched the bartender, and she never said a word; she just listened to Mom. What could she do? I asked Mom if we could leave. I wasn't scared to talk to her now, because as a teenager, I had gotten stronger in my own emotions. Besides, I was used to her hitting and vicious words.

Her laughter had changed now; it was loud, and she couldn't quit. She would go into a fit of laughter and not be able to stop, but she would be looking at people when she did it. It made other people really uncomfortable. They'd look confused, but no one said anything. Everyone just looked away. She refused to leave until she'd had a couple of beers. I could tell by the way people looked at Mom that this wasn't the first time she had been in there and done that, and I was grateful I didn't have to come with her every time.

Mom began to resent my grandma, her mother. There was a hate in her eyes that was beginning to show. I would watch when we stopped at Grandma's house. Mom verbally abused my grandma; she said things that made no sense at all. "You think they are on your side, but they are not!"

"You're talking crazy. Evelyn, you're getting sick again." Grandma's response always made it worse. She had no idea how to deal with having a mentally ill daughter. I looked at Grandma's face, and I could see the pain and the tears building in her eyes.

Weeks later, Grandma called Dad. "Come to my house right away!" she screamed.

Mom had driven to Grandma's house, but when we got there, Mom was gone.

Grandma was crying and shaking.

"What the heck happened here?" Dad asked.

Grandma told Dad that Mom barged in, saying things that made no sense. She accused Grandma of hurting her and her brother, and said that Grandma was crazy in the head. She kept saying to Grandma that people have been watching her for some time now. Mom yelled at her, and when Grandma tried to stop her, Mom reached in the cupboard and grabbed one of the big butcher knives.

"You make me so mad," Mom had said.

When Grandma realized Mom wasn't going to put down the knife, she ran outside to her outdoor patio building and locked herself inside. "I was so scared she was going to hurt me with the knife. I stayed in the patio house until I saw her car leave."

Before Mom took off, she dumped a whole bag of flour all over the kitchen cupboards and floor. She trashed the living room. She'd made a horrible mess. Dad and Grandma looked at the knife and knew this time Mom's mind had gone to a darker side. Dad said, "I've got to get her to the mental institution as soon as possible." The worry on his face and the hurt and pain hung over him like a cloud. He looked at Grandma and said, "How am I going to get her there?"

Dad talked to me like I was an adult. "We are in this together," he said. "You have to help me take care of things." My role was changing. I would no longer be a child, and at fifteen, I was taking on the responsibilities of a grown-up. "We have to get your mom some help," Dad said as he stood by the doorway, looking out the back door. His voice began to quiver, and the words penetrated my mind as he said, "I wonder if Mom would have hurt Grandma today."

We helped Grandma clean up the house, and when we got back home, Mom was nowhere to be found. There was a knock on our door. I looked at the uniform and wondered why the sheriff was standing on our front step. We hadn't done anything wrong. I looked at his badge, and all of a sudden, my mind took me back to the sheriff at the mental center years ago.

I heard the sheriff tell my dad how dangerous it had been with Evelyn driving the wrong way down streets in town. "She could have caused a serious accident. People around town feel badly, but they are scared of what she might do," he told Dad. "You need to take her to the mental institution today. You have to commit her today, or I will take her in the police car and do it myself."

I was listening to my father have to apologize. He told the sheriff, "She doesn't mean anything. She's just sick. I will get her brother, and he will help me take her." I could tell the sheriff was a nice man. He seemed to understand.

I can't imagine the pain and embarrassment my father must have felt. He loved his wife. The illness had brought about a huge financial burden. It had also put Mom's mental illness front and center to all who knew our family. Dad had moved us back to the place where Mom had grown up. Her folks also grew up there, as did several other generations of her family. My father had many generations of family that had grown up there, too. They'd gone to the same school. Mom started her teaching career in Burwell. They were married in Burwell. I was born in Burwell. Everyone for generations knew each other. I couldn't tell if these roots were support for my dad or a cause of embarrassment. He never complained or told anyone how he felt; he just kept busy and dealt with helping Mom. He held strong.

The day was about to get long. Was there hate? Yes, so much it hurt. We hated mental illness and the fact that it was taking our mom away. It was so hard to understand the sickness. There was no blood or cuts or physical signs. Mom looked fine. I wished someone could have explained to me what was happening. All that anyone seemed able to do was medicate her. They gave her so many drugs and said if they didn't work, she could live in an institution surrounded by other people who were mentally ill. The solution being proposed was to hide her from the world, simply because no one knew how to heal the brain.

In 1955, state mental institutions in the U.S. housed nearly 560,000 patients, of which my mom was one.

I think of her illness all the time. If my mother would have had her illness today, she wouldn't have spent so much time in and out of institutions. Nowadays, people struggling with mental illness, including schizophrenia, can have treatment and live at home.

By 1977, because of a bill signed by John F. Kennedy just one month before his death, U.S. mental institutions had reduced their collective population to only about 160,000 people. He signed the Community Mental Health Center Act of 1963, which provided $150 million to free thousands of mentally ill Americans from their lives in institutions. The bill envisioned building 1,500 outpatient mental health centers to offer people community-based care instead.

Mom came home, and Dad never said a thing. She said she wanted to lie down on the couch for a while; she was tired. Dad said, "Your brother is coming over; he needs to borrow some tools." Mom fell asleep.

I went to my bedroom wondering what was going to happen. In some ways, I felt sorry for my mother. Eventually, Dad and my uncle came into the house. My uncle went into the living room to talk with his sister.

Meanwhile, Dad came into my room, shut the door, and said, "You have to pack some clothes for your mom. Everything she will need for a long time." I didn't say anything, but I could feel the blood start to leave me as if my heart was slowing down. It was killing me. I hated the fact that Mom was sick. I knew she had to go, but I wanted the sickness to end. Why couldn't someone help her? I looked at my father, his face twisted with sadness. His large, tough farm hands were shaking.

"Put the suitcase in the trunk of your uncle's car, the keys are in it. We will keep Mom in the living room." I grabbed the suitcase and went into their bedroom and started packing her clothes. I looked in her dresser drawers. I didn't know what she might like. I felt like she was dead, and I was taking her things. I was mixed up. I could barely see past my own tears. I wanted to cry out, but I knew I had to stay quiet. I put in underwear and bras, and for some reason, I even put in Kotex pads. I put in the blouses I liked best on her, and I packed her favorite shoes even though I thought they were ugly. I knew she liked them. I stopped for a minute and smelled the last blouse before putting it in the suitcase. I wanted to hold her, but I couldn't. It was as though my mother was dying. I was used to her mental illness by now. I wondered why anyone would put her back into that spooky old building. I hugged her blouse again. Her perfume was strong, and the scent helped me. I put some of her makeup in the suitcase, too. I knew from past visits to the ward that Mom had asked Dad to bring her makeup. She always wore makeup. She said there was no excuse to look bad, even if you do live on a farm. I finished packing her bag.

I wanted to put our family picture in the suitcase, but Dad had told me patients couldn't have anything with glass. I walked quietly down the hallway. I glanced at the back of my mother, the person who didn't like me, who said I was dumb. Feeling sick, I got past the living room and put the suitcase in the trunk.

When I went back into the house, I could hear the conversation among Dad, my uncle, and Mom. I realized they had to trick my mom to go with them. Mom would say, "Richard, you're the one who is sick. You know you're crazy. You're so stupid, you don't even know how much everyone is laughing at you."

Dad would agree. "You're right, let's all go to the doctor. If he says I am sick, I will stay, and you and your brother can leave me there."

I was standing by the sink doing dishes when my father said, "We will be going now."

"I will be back," Mom said.

Dad touched my shoulder on the way out. "It will be okay."

After they left, I fell down to the floor and cried until my insides hurt. I hated this pattern, and now Mom was gone again. *When will it end?* The tears didn't stop. I felt like I could have cried for days. Then a cold, firm feeling hit me. I didn't want to give in to pain. I got up and realized Dad and my siblings needed me. I put myself into overdrive, cleaning and doing laundry, making sure every task was done. It was like a switch went off in my mind. I was no longer a child. Overnight, I became an adult. In the back of my mind, I was thinking how much Mom would hate me. *She will see her suitcase and the clothes, and she will know it was me.*

Life pressed on. Dad continued to work hard. My brother helped Dad every day. I kept the house clean. My sister was still so young, she often went to play with the neighbor girl. They were good friends. It was summer now, and I helped Dad out on the farm, too. We were always together with Dad. We visited Mom on the weekends. It was getting difficult for me to watch her cry when we left. I acted like an adult at home, but my heart was broken. I couldn't stand Mom when she treated me badly, but I also couldn't stand it when she was gone. She did care for us. She cooked meals. She washed our clothes. And when she wasn't paranoid, she was a solid presence in the house: an adult who was there if we needed her.

I missed not having a mom in my life. I hated the thought I wasn't doing what other young girls were getting to do. They were at sport camps or on vacations with their families. I sat on a step around the side of the house where no one could see me. I held one of my cats and thought about when we were younger. We did get a few great vacations with Mom. We went to the mountains in Colorado, and I got to feed a chipmunk. Grandma had come along, and we stopped in parks for picnics. Mom seemed to enjoy all of us. I wished for the days when we used to go shopping for clothes and spend whole afternoons looking through the catalog at all the new fashions. I missed dressing chickens with Mom and Grandma. I didn't like the mess, but I loved listening to their stories. Then my mind would go quiet. I'd run out of thoughts and be back in my world once again.

Then Mom would come home. And once again, our lives would be altered by a mind that was subject to schizophrenia. I'd long for the Sundays when Dad, my siblings, and I had free time. Maybe Dad knew what we were all going through, so he'd give us all—including himself—a break. We loved Sundays in the pickup with Dad.

As we traveled to the pastures to check on the cows, we would listen to the radio to the *Big Joe Polka Show*. The waltzes and polkas spoke to our Bohemian roots, and we laughed and bounced our way across the hills, seeing the cows and baby calves, savoring the sounds of the music that soothed our wounded souls. Listening to polka music became a sanctuary, as holy as any church. It was the sweetest, calmest time of my life. The world stopped, and for those fleeting moments, I felt love, and had a heck of a lot of fun.

Dad let my sister and I join the Burwell Saddle Club. Dad would load our horses in the trailer, and we would go to competitions. There was barrel racing, pole bending, and sack racing. If you won, you got a ribbon. I got a lot of ribbons over those summers. When I got a little older, I had summer jobs and had to quit going. My sister went with Dad many summers to come, and she won a lot of trophies and dozens of ribbons.

In the summer evenings, my brother, sister, and I would run in the dark and catch lightning bugs. We would wait until Mom and Dad were asleep, and we would quietly sneak outside, where we'd stay for hours. We each had a mason jar and a lid, and we made holes in the top for air. We each got at least five bugs apiece and put them in our jars with grass for them to eat. As I ran through the darkness with the summer breeze blowing through my hair, I felt free. There was no weight on my chest. No yelling. We would put the jars in our bedroom windows and watch the lightning bugs emit their light. It was truly amazing.

We used to pile into Dad's pickup to make sure all the bulls were in the pasture. Once, Dad saw a bull and couldn't tell if it was old number nine (the one that would chase us), so he got out of the pickup and walked up to it. He wanted the bull to turn so he could see his ear tag. About that time, the bull did turn and started charging toward Dad. There was a small ditch between Dad and the pickup, and as he ran toward the truck, he tripped. He was on his knees, trying to crawl fast to get to safety. My little sister, who was sitting by his door, panicked at seeing the bull coming toward the truck, so she reached over and pulled the door shut. Dad yelled, "Jesus Christ!" and dove under the pickup to avoid being gored by the bull. My brother and I wanted to laugh, but we were scared Dad would get mad at us. He finally got out from under the truck, jumped in, and said, "Why in the hell did you shut the door?" My sister explained that she didn't want the bull to get her. What could he say? He began to laugh, and then we all joined in, laughing until our sides hurt.

FEAR OF LOSING DAD

Mom was home now and seemed to want to sleep all afternoon.

There was always plenty for us to do outside. One afternoon, we were helping Dad chase pigs into a trailer so he could get them to another pen. Getting big feeder pigs to go down an alleyway into a trailer is no easy chore. If they decide to turn around and bolt past you, they just do.

We were fighting to get the pigs loaded. Dad had an electric wire that was high above the alleyway and ran the length of the alley to another pen.

We almost had all the pigs in the trailer when they turned around and bolted out, coming right for Dad. He scrambled to get up the fence so they wouldn't knock him down. The twenty pigs coming at him weighed over two hundred pounds each. He got to the top of the fence, then let out the most horrifying yell. We all looked at him, and his head dropped. It looked like he was going to fall down. He grabbed the fence hard to hang on. I watched him reach for his forehead, rubbing it. When he looked up at us, I could see the severe red line across his forehead. He had touched his head on the electric wire.

When he turned to look at us, his face was milky white and somewhat gray. My heart raced. *Dad, don't die! I can't be with Mom without you!* I thought. He sat for a while.

"Are you okay, Dad?"

"Get them damn pigs running back here; let's do this again," he said, and his tone of voice had such strength.

We chased them back down the alleyway, and it was like they knew, "Don't mess with this man!"

I was relieved when the day was done. I just kept thinking, *Don't ever die, Dad, I need you.*

Fall came, and the school year started up once again. There was no way I was going to allow friends to visit me at my house. I still never told them anything about my mom. I didn't want kids making fun of my family.

Mom was back from the institution, but she'd already begun to slide. This time, it was worse. She'd take her medication, but then she would drink, sometimes heavily. After school, I would come home, and Mom would be passed out on the couch. A six-pack sitting amid her medication, evidence of her comatose state. Amazingly, she would wake up around four thirty and work to get supper on the table. She would walk around, constantly chewing on ice. The crunching was loud and annoying.

She could look at me as if she were seeing right through me. I saw nothing in her face except disgust and hate. It wouldn't be long, and the hurtful words would come. For the most part, I was growing up in silence, peppered with toxic insults that tore me down. I could say to myself over and over, *Mom's just sick.*

She can't help it. In reality, it still affected how I felt about myself. I had heard the words so many times. I just believed them. I was getting tired of all the negative feelings, but I couldn't do anything to fix them. It seemed to me Mom was changing, but it wasn't for the better. It was just different. I realized she would never be well, that *this* woman would always be my mom.

Walking into the house after school gave me butterflies, because I never knew what I would encounter. I knew other girls went home to moms who hugged them and talked to them.

Why couldn't my mom hug me? Why did she not want to hug me? I tried not to say anything, because angry words would always bounce back at me. The verbal abuse made our whole house a nightmare. It had become my mission to hide my mom's craziness as much as I could.

Now that I was in high school, I made a few good friends, one right off the bat. She had a brother who was much older than we were. It was as if she were the only child, so she asked me to stay overnight with her a lot.

Sometimes, we stayed at her grandma's in town. I would do anything to not lose my friend. I really liked her and would do whatever she wanted. Frequently, we would sneak out of her basement window at night and go uptown to see her boyfriend.

I found myself wishing I had someone special. I promised to keep her escapades a secret. We never went to my place. I said it wouldn't be as fun because I had a little brother and sister who wouldn't leave us alone. That line always seemed to work. When we went to her home in the country, it was quiet. Everyone spoke so softly. I clung to my new friend and some other girls. I wanted what they had. I desperately wanted their "normal." I never wanted school days to end.

On weekends, Dad let us drive the tractors and the pickup. He taught us when we were young. Sometimes, I drove our little International 300 tractor down the lane to the river. There was something about this that was freeing for me. I loved making the tractor go as fast as it could. It was such a teenage moment.

Sometimes on Saturday nights, he took Mom out to dinner. I enjoyed this time of being alone. Even if my brother and sister were there, I felt alone, and it was wonderful. Over time, those date nights became infrequent until, ultimately, they ended. I then felt more and more trapped and isolated from the rest of the world.

Pleasing others and trying to be perfect became my coping mechanisms. If I could only be my best, then maybe I could make everything okay at home. If I could just please my parents enough, maybe I could make Mom better and fix all that was wrong with our family.

When Mom and Dad said they would be gone for the day, I was elated. On these days, I decided I was going to make my mother better. I was determined to look great in their eyes. One time, I cleaned the whole basement. I wanted it to be beautiful when they returned home. I was driven to please my parents and to hear the words, "We are so proud of you! Thanks so much!" I scrubbed every inch of the cement floor. In my mind, I kept hearing Mom say, "You did such a wonderful job. I love you." I thought about this the whole time I cleaned.

I came across a big trash can full of papers. I thought it must have been paperwork from Dad's desk that he hadn't yet bothered to throw away or take to the burn barrel. We burned our own garbage on the farm. I wondered why none of the papers were crumpled up. They were all lying flat. It was difficult to carry the huge trash can up the stairs from the basement. I had to lift with all my might, one step at a time. Finally, after struggling with it, I managed to get it outside to the burn barrels. I knew it would take forever to burn, so I got some gasoline. I put papers in the barrel, lit them, and kept adding more until the papers were all in and burning. This alone took about two hours. I was proud of myself for cleaning the basement; it was spotless.

I was exhausted, but I had so much excitement inside. I knew Mom and Dad would be amazed. So as soon as they walked into the house, I told them to go to the basement because I had a surprise. I waited at the top of the steps, and Mom and Dad went downstairs. I was expecting glowing praise, but what I got instead was an agonizing scream from my dad. "Oh my God, where are all my papers? Oh my God!" I had never heard him yell like that. It sounded like he was crying at the same time. With dread, I listened to what Dad told Mom, "Look what she did! She burned all the tax papers, which are required to be saved for seven years!" It seemed like he was down there for a long time and couldn't even come upstairs to look at me. I was overcome with a cold, sick feeling.

My dad would have to live in fear for the next three or four years until the time elapsed on those papers. He sounded as though he was crying again. "What if we get audited?" My sincere desire to please them hadn't worked out like I had expected. Not one word was said about how clean the basement looked.

In the midst of living with a mom who couldn't show love for me, who constantly berated me, I unwittingly ended up doing a "stupid" thing. Mom went off about how stupid I was, telling my dad, "See, Richard, we have raised a dumbbell." The weight I felt at that moment was unbearable; I had given my dad a reason to hate me, to think I really *was* dumb.

HIGH SCHOOL

D ad said we could join only one activity at school. My
salvation was joining the volleyball team. This gave
me an after-school activity with workouts and time
with my friends. We'd bus to other towns for games. I was playing well with my two best girlfriends. The three of us were close
and always sat together on the bus.

One afternoon, we were coming back from a game, and on
the highway, the bus driver passed an old farmer on a little red
tractor. The three of us decided to moon him. We dropped our
pants and put our butts in the back window of the bus, giving the
old man on the tractor quite a view. We all laughed, including the
rest of our team. We figured we were fine; we had gotten away with
it. The coach didn't see it; all was good with the world. Then some-
body ratted on us. The coach was furious; she told everyone that
to decide on an appropriate punishment, there would be a man-
datory meeting with all of us and our parents after school the next
day. We were terrified. The first thing I thought of was my mom.

My mother's illness had shifted again. Now, she would ex-
plode at any time, and it would last for hours before she'd return

to normal. It would happen without warning. I was praying this would not make her go nuts or say embarrassing things at my school. I didn't want anyone at the school to know about her.

The meeting was at five o'clock on Friday afternoon. I sat in the front of the room with my mischief-making friends, worrying about whether Mom would keep it together. *Would she completely lose her grip on reality?*

I wanted to lie to Mom and not let her know there was a school meeting, but I knew it wouldn't work, since the school called all the parents. My heart raced. *Please, God, don't let her do it here!*

I was sitting quietly when my mom stood up. *Oh Lord,* I thought, *do I run out of here? What am I going to do?* As Mom stood there, the coach, who was sitting by the principal and other people from the school board, asked, "Evelyn, do you have an opinion on this matter? We will let you go first since you're standing."

Her voice was humorous. "I feel it was just bare butts, and with everything that is going on in this world today, I do not think we need to be concerned about three bare butts."

Every parent in the room laughed. I could not believe what she said next: "I think that we need to press on and get into something that is a bit more serious. The girls know they did wrong. Maybe they should sit out one game. Let's all go home and get back to living."

I was so proud of her that day! I went home and said, "Gosh, Mom, that was great." I looked at her, thinking how much I really liked her. It was so special how she'd protected me at school. It was so easy to like her at these moments because the bad days outweighed them by so many. I thought I would get a break and, for a split second, see the mom I so desperately wanted. No more than one moment later, I received a pulverizing hit on the side of my head.

"You are so damn stupid. I can't believe you're my kid. You do not belong to me. You are your dad's daughter. You are so stupid to act like that in front of people. They are making fun of you! Damn stupid kid. Why would you pull me into that school?"

I instantly lost everything all over again. The mean Mom was back with a vengeance. I went to my room, shut the door, certain I couldn't deal with it anymore. I was fighting feelings of hate. I didn't want to hate, but I did hate. I really did not like Mom anymore. I wished I were somewhere else. I was envious of my girlfriends. I wanted to leave right then. I couldn't wait until Monday morning so I could return to school and be with my friends. I hated home.

Monday came, and my friends and I drove around on our lunch hour. We listened to Paul Harvey on the radio, ate Fritos with ketchup on them, and treated ourselves to frozen Snickers bars. It was this small fragment of time each day that I cherished.

I did crazy things like power burnouts with my '65 Impala. A power burnout required holding my foot hard on the brake and then stepping on the gas until the engine raced. I then shoved the car into reverse so the tires squealed and spun, leaving rubber marks in the shape of fish hooks on the pavement of the school parking lot. I did this almost every lunch hour.

I was getting wonderful attention, not from the principal but from the kids who always stood outside until the bell rang. They loved it. I was almost becoming the class clown. I felt adulation from the whole student body. Everything was wonderful until it was time to go home.

As I drove my brother and myself home, the lights of my fun and joy switched off one by one. It was as though we walked into an enveloping sadness in the evening.

One of my girlfriends called me on the phone to chat. I could hear Mom yelling, so I told her I needed to go do chores and quickly hung up. I didn't want anyone, especially my friend, to hear my mother's tirades.

I felt her body near my back, and the goose pimples rose on my neck. "Who were you talking to?"

"I was talking with Cindy."

"Sure you were, you goddamn dumbbell. You got some secrets."

As I turned around and looked at her, my skin began to crawl. There was nowhere to go. I couldn't get words to come out of my throat. I knew I had to get past her, to go outside and get away. My body began to tighten. I took a deep breath. I made it past her without being hit.

I started walking down our dirt road that led to the river. I knew where to go: my favorite place along the riverbank. I could feel the water rush through my toes as I sat and stared at the sun glaring off the surface of the water. I started thinking of the endless excuses I'd found for why my friends couldn't come stay over at my house. Then, out of the blue, came a wonderful idea.

I decided to have a little party for my four girlfriends. It started out as no big deal. The plan was just to have a few girlfriends over to camp out by the river. I wanted them to be with me, but not to see my mom. We planned to have some beer and a little wine. One of the girls knew someone who could get us booze. We took the cooler of booze down to the campsite and hid it behind some trees.

I was supposed to pick up each girl and her sleeping bag after school. The Four Musketeers were set to have a fun Friday night camp-out, drinking and having some laughs. Everything seemed to be going well.

However, my little brother had spied on us, watching me take the cooler of booze down to the river that afternoon. Needless to say, when we were down at our campsite, he was ratting us out. One of the girls had also told a bunch of other people about the party. My little evening of fun was about to get out of control.

I saw car lights coming down our lane. I saw flashlights and heard laughter and yelling coming from across my father's alfalfa field. I heard what sounded like hundreds of people wading across the river, splashing water, like rafts coming toward the bank. *Oh, God!* I thought. *I am going to be killed!* I had no idea who all the people crashing our party were. I could hear their laughter, and I didn't know how to stop them from coming.

This can't be happening to me! Then I saw a huge spotlight and heard my dad's loud voice, "You'd better get out of that tree. You all had better go home."

Later, I found out a classmate of mine was up in a tree trying to hide from my father. Kids were running away, looking for places to hide. It took my dad hours to get everyone off our property. The four of us just stood by our campfire, scared shitless.

They had no idea about my mother or the relationship we shared. I wanted to run, but where would I go? Dad kept his cool in front of my friends. My brother was sitting in the truck beside him, smiling his shit-ass grin. "You girls load your stuff, and get in the car. Come to the house. You will be spending the rest of the night inside." As we lay on the floor, I told them I didn't want to take them home in the morning.

I dropped them off, one by one, and drove very slowly home. I walked in and went straight to my bedroom to find my family sitting on my bed. Dad proceeded to tell me how disappointed he was in me and how irresponsible I'd been. He said I didn't have to worry about the rest of the summer, because I would be working on the farm and not going anywhere. I was grounded. I thought I was going to die. At the same time, I was happy I wasn't getting hit. I don't know why Mom was quiet. She just stared at me with no emotion. I could tell Dad was very upset.

The natural part of being a teenager was beginning to happen. Boys were flirting, and my friends were dating. I was in a new phase of life. One young man was always saying hi to me. He was a year older, so of course that was cool. There was a part of me that was interested in having a boyfriend. I was looking forward to the possibility of getting attention.

The boy lived right down the road from our farm. His family had a few acres. Young courtship grew between us. I asked permission to date.

"You have to be home at ten o'clock, and if you go anywhere, it's just into town for a little while."

I wasn't given total freedom, but I loved having somewhere to go every Saturday night. I was getting all the extra attention I needed. I had no idea how starved for hugs I'd been or what hearing kind words would do to me. I never said anything to disagree with my boyfriend. I didn't want to lose him because I loved the freedom and attention that came from dating.

I would find reasons to go over to his house. I was growing fond of his mother, and I liked not having the yelling, the looks, or the feeling that I was no better than dirt. I was hoping this would go on forever, but Mom's sickness wouldn't allow it.

At this time, her treatment plan consisted of a few beers and her prescribed pills. It was like a blessing when she slept. Dad was so exhausted that having Mom asleep for most of the day was just fine with him. All the bills from her treatments still weighed heavily on my father. The health insurance didn't cover mental illness, so the burden was his alone.

I was carrying laundry downstairs when I found Mom standing by the washing machine, smelling my underwear. I was shocked. *God, you're sick,* I thought, though I never said a word. Mom looked at me with such a sour expression.

"I don't want any papooses running around here for me to watch! I am going to make sure!" I couldn't believe what I was hearing. Was Mom referring to babies? Was she saying I was going to get pregnant? I didn't think Mom could get any worse, but then she looked at me like she looked at Dad: no warm thoughts. Just a sickened stare that went right through me. "I am going to put you on the pill."

I took off running outside. I don't know if I was scared of the word *pill,* or I thought it would be something that could hurt me. I ran until I found Dad. He was dirty from working in the fields. I could tell he was tired, but that didn't stop me. "Mom is going to put me on the pill, Dad. What is that?"

I couldn't tell him Mom was smelling my underwear. I just wanted some kind of reassurance. As I turned, Mom was right there, and she went to slap me. Dad said, "Stop hitting her, for God's sake. What is going on here? What is the deal with a pill?"

"You had to run to your dad, didn't you? That's right, tell your dad, you damn dumbbell."

The three of us walked toward the house. I wasn't sure what would happen next. We went in. Dad drank a glass of water, turned around, and went back outside.

"You damn dumbbell. You're so stupid. I need to take care of this problem; your dad doesn't know anything!" I was old enough now to know the drill. If I went along with her thoughts, no matter what she said, I would get the kinder side of Mom.

I was too scared to say anything. I just stayed out of everyone's view. I went down by the river and walked around. I tried to plan out what to say. Part of my survivor side said, *Go on the pill; it's not going to hurt you, and it will make points with Mom. Do you want to be hit some more or yelled at some more? Play the game. You're not a dumbbell. Play the game.*

The next morning, I became someone I had created in my mind, a survivor. Someone who knew how to play the game, to act like I agreed with everything Mom dreamed up. I was going to pretend to be whoever Mom wanted me to be, just as I had done with my friends and others my whole life.

I waited until the afternoon when I knew Dad was out of the house. My brother and sister were somewhere else. I went to Mom, looked at her, and said, "You're right, I should be on the pill. I am sorry. I am a dumbbell." I will never forget the look she gave me . . . It was as if she was saying, "You are finally admitting you're an idiot, and I have to help you."

That week, Mom took me to the doctor and demanded I be put on the pill. I just sat there and listened to my mom tell the doctor about me and how stupid I was, and that she didn't want a papoose coming, which could happen, because I was dumb.

I didn't realize I was about to get my first Pap smear. I didn't like what this man was about to do. The idea of an instrument being inserted into me scared me. He told me it would hurt. This instantly took me back to the time I was told to hold a cock. I couldn't escape this time either. Just the idea of taking my pants off and being examined was shocking. Thank goodness there was a nurse there. She never said anything to me, but I felt her kindness and understanding. I had less cause for shame with her there.

Nothing was said on the drive to the pharmacy. Mom left me in the car and went inside to get the pills. I just sat there in silence, thinking, *This is my new role. I have to be the person Mom wants no matter what is going on in my head or how much I want to scream at the top of my lungs, "Someone please help me. What is happening here?"* Suddenly, the thought of not being here went racing through my mind once again. The feeling of not being loved was almost too much for me to bear.

At home, Mom made supper as if nothing had happened. No big deal, I'd take a little pill. The whole experience was making me feel dirty. I wondered why Dad hadn't helped me. I was at a new level of pain from my mother. Now, she was making me go places and let other people hurt me.

My whole body felt cold as ice. I just wanted to disappear. I had no sense of belonging.

Dad and Mom took turns going into town to check on Grandma Mary. Dad had just put Grandma in the hospital and told us at the dinner table she wasn't feeling very well. That night I was trying to fall asleep when the phone rang. I heard my dad talking quietly. I couldn't make out what he was saying. Then everything was quiet. I leaned up in bed, and I could hear a strange sound coming from the living room. I opened our bedroom door so I could figure out what was going on. I stepped out in the hallway, and I could see the shadow of my dad. He had his face buried in his hands and was crying. His body shook. I had never seen my dad cry.

"What are you doing up?" Mom said. I watched her ask Dad if he was all right. His face never lifted from his hands. "Mom's gone." In a few days, Dad told us Grandma was ready for friends and family to come say good-bye. She was at the funeral home for viewing. That afternoon, I went alone to the funeral home, relieved no one else was there. I went inside to see my grandma and to tell her I loved her. As I looked at her, I wondered if she knew about our homelife. For years, Dad had not brought her out to the house. Tears ran down my face thinking of all the times she and Grandpa Frank had taken care of me. For those short periods in my life, they'd given me a break.

I became a workaholic outside with my dad. It wasn't just by choice. Dad needed help, and I needed to stay outside. It was my job to vaccinate all the baby pigs and clip their baby teeth so they wouldn't chew up the mama sow's nipples. The worst part was getting the mama sow out of the pen and locking the door so she couldn't get back inside. The sows would hear the baby pigs squeal when I worked on them, and they would snort loudly, like they wanted to eat me for lunch.

Sometimes, from the seat of a tractor or a pickup, I watched my sister backing out the car that Mom had given her, playing music loudly on the tape deck. Michael Jackson's "Beat It" was her favorite. The car was a beautiful red Vega with a white interior. It had been Mom's car, but Mom bought a new car, so my sister got to have hers. My sister was my mom's biggest joy.

Mom never treated her the way she treated me. It was becoming more and more challenging to take, because I wondered why my sister did not get yelled at, why she was never called a dumbbell and didn't get hit. I kept trying to rationalize things. I told myself it was because of Mom's sickness. She had schizophrenia and severe manic delusions, whatever the hell that meant.

I worked this over and over in my mind, and it would often consume my thinking. I talked to myself. "When she gets bad, she hates me, she hates Grandma, she hates Dad, but why can she constantly love my sister and not be upset with her?" Mom was a different person around her. Her facial expression would even change if I approached them.

I was playing my role the best I could; acting became easy for me, but it was taking a toll.

I needed to escape the bubble I lived in.

It wasn't difficult to do what the other kids were doing. I was all in. I started drinking, getting drunk, and puking before I went home. I had my first sexual encounter. It was with the first boyfriend I had. "I think you're very pretty," he said. He always had his arm around me or held my hand. I enjoyed flirting with him. The attention he gave me was an incredible feeling. I loved the feeling of being wanted. One evening, we started kissing and he slid his hand inside my jeans. I could feel the button letting go, and as I heard the zipper sliding down, I began to get scared. I didn't want him to stop liking me. I didn't want to lose his affection. There were so many thoughts going off in my head. *You'd better not do this. What if someone comes home and catches us?* As my mind raced, I realized my pants were off. I felt him lying on me, grinding his penis into my abdomen, whispering, "I want you," over and over in my ear. The passion of all this overwhelmed me, and I reached down and slid my panties lower so he could enter me. I could feel the head of the penis pushing hard between my legs, and it felt like my skin was closed.

As he held on to his dick and continued to try to guide it into my body, it just wasn't working. Finally, he started to enter me, and the pain was intense. I asked him to stop because it hurt so badly. I didn't know what to say. He started rubbing up and down on my pubic bone as though he was still fucking me. He exploded cum all over my stomach. I didn't like the smell of him. I was so relieved it was over. He smiled at me like it was no big deal and said, "We'd better get cleaned up." I hurried and picked up my clothes and went into the bathroom. I looked in the mirror at myself and the thought of being loved and wanted was so wonderful, but the sex didn't please me at all. I wondered if I would always have to do this to be loved. *If that's what it takes, so be it.* I figured if Mom wanted me on the pill, this must be what she was expecting me to do. I started to feel so ashamed of myself. Coldness came over me as I thought of my mom.

Starving for affection, never being able to say, "No," became my way. I had no strength at this time to stand up for myself. Whatever anyone wanted to do with me, I went along with it. I wanted to feel loved; I wanted to know someone wanted me, so all attention, no matter what kind, I took. I became wild, and it wasn't just having sex, it was going to parties, going to pool halls, playing foosball. It didn't matter. Wherever my friends went, I went, as long as it wasn't home.

Mom let us have nice clothes. We were a comparatively wealthy family, so dressing well came easy. I loved clothes. I started to hear girls say how attractive I looked, and I realized this was going to help fill my void.

The boy I was dating was getting attached to me. If he only knew I wasn't in my right mind anymore. I played the game at home and with my friends to get their acceptance and be liked. Inside my body and mind, I was emotionally wasted. I didn't feel a thing, and I realized it didn't bug me. People may have thought, *Wow, she loves the guy,* and so on. But that wasn't it; I was just fueling my need for touch and affection, getting my fix before I went home.

I was getting good at being the "Karen" someone needed at any given moment. I started shutting my mother off at this point. When she called me names and did everything she normally did to me, I just turned the volume down.

I could be in the bathtub getting ready for a Saturday-night date, and Mom would come in and hit my naked body with the handle end of the flyswatter.

"You're so dumb, you'd better behave when you go out." She would work herself into a rage thinking she needed to beat me. I sat in the tub aware that the first hit would sting, but then I'd go into a zone of oblivion. No matter how many times she hit me, I'd feel nothing.

Then she would just stand there and stare at me, until I yelled, "Get out of here!" When the door closed, I saw the welts on my arm. I hurried and finished so I could get my clothes on. I couldn't wait to leave the house, even if it was only a few hours.

This carried through my whole high school life. I could shut down emotionally and not feel things. I became quieter and quieter. I was still a loving person to everyone, but inside, I could feel a shield coming over me. Now that I was getting older, I was going to have to protect myself from everybody. *Don't let them into your heart and space.*

POPULAR

I was popular in school; everyone, apart from one teacher, seemed to like me. I think her contempt came from her son liking me. She didn't want us to date. I blew her off, thinking to myself she was just a mean old lady, no different from Mom. I entered her classroom and prayed the forty-five minutes would go by fast.

She assigned a book report. We were supposed to come up with our own story. The story was supposed to be from real life, but written as a childhood fairy tale. I thought of *The Three Bears,* and I made it about Watergate. I worked hard on it.

My mom wasn't interested, even though she had been a great teacher. "I don't need to read it. You won't get a good grade anyway. You're just a dumbbell."

I shared it with my aunt, who loved it. "You should get a good grade on this," she said.

The day came to read it aloud in class. The teacher said she was recording everyone's stories so we could listen back and see how they sounded. It was my turn to read. When I finished, the kids clapped. They seemed to love it. The teacher didn't say a word. She just played the tape. I didn't know that when a person is nervous, their voice can become shaky. It sounded like I was stuttering. I didn't hear it with the naked ear. Some of my classmates laughed or giggled. I sat down in my seat, not knowing how to react. I could feel my face getting hot, and I knew it must have turned red.

The teacher stood up and accused me of getting help with my work. She said, "There is no way you came up with this yourself. Someone helped you." I was mortified. She graded us right on the spot. She told me, "It's an A paper, but I will give you a B." She wrote on the paper, "Tell whoever helped you, 'Great job.'"

I was angry! I thought, *You're just like my mom. I know you.* The next classmate got up and started reading his story. I was filled with mixed emotions after having been belittled.

At this time, in the seventies, midriff tops were popular. They were blouses that came barely to the top of your jeans. If you sat down, a half inch of your back would show.

My seat was in the very back row. I heard the teacher walking behind me while the boy was still reading his story. All at once, I could feel her finger slide across the bare part of my back. I was stunned, scared, and mad. I wanted to scream at her and ask her what her problem was, but that was the girl inside. The one on the outside was a shell—scared and quiet. All I did was turn red. Some of the other kids saw her do it and asked me after class, "Wow, how are you? She must hate your guts for some reason."

I was in shock. My stomach hurt. I didn't want to be dumb, but when called that so much, a person begins to believe it.

I knew my work was good. Why was the teacher treating me like my mother did? She all but called me dumb in front of the class. I hated her. I couldn't wait to pass and be done with her class.

I was trying so hard to be successful in school. Years earlier, I spent a lot of time in my room playing records. I pretended I was singing, looking at myself in the mirror. My favorite record was by the singer Barbara Mandrell. I would fantasize about being her and escape to that world in my mind. I did this for years.

One day, I looked in the mirror, and I didn't like me anymore. The pretending quit working. I was ashamed, like I could see myself, but I couldn't feel me. I thought, *You will never be able to sing. You are not the next Barbara Mandrell.*

I joined a music class with my friends because I still had the desire to sing. We hadn't been in class long, and the teacher said, "There is someone in here who can't carry a note." He went around the group and had each person sing. He got in front of me and asked me to sing. I did. I thought I sounded great. "It's you," he said.

I figured, since he was the teacher, he should teach me how to sing. He said he didn't have time to teach me, and he wanted me to take a different class during this hour. He sent me to home economics class that very minute. He had no idea how much it hurt me. I was damaged already, and these hurts continued to pile up. It made me so upset that instead of going to home ec, I got a ladder from the janitor's room and some balloons from my locker. I filled them with water and used the ladder to put them on the door hinge above the music room. I knew that the teacher always came out of the door first, and he would be hit in the head with the water balloon. I waited and hid behind the wall to watch the explosion of water. I was going to get my payback on him for ruining my singing career. The bell rang to end the class. He came flying out and boom! Right on his head. Water everywhere. The next thing I knew, I was sitting in the principal's office. He told me how wrong that was, but inside my heart and mind, I kept thinking, *No, it's not. He ruined my dream. I wanted to sing.*

I hated going to home ec. I already knew how to cook and clean. My grandma loved it, because I had to make a dress and two pillows, and I needed her help. She was an excellent seamstress. This meant I would spend time with her, and I knew she was lonely. For this reason alone, home ec was a good thing, even though I wanted to sing like Barbara Mandrell.

One day, I decided to agree with Mom and say stupid things such as, "Flowers do need to be yellow. A leaf does need to point in a certain direction."

Mom began to respond to me, not positively yet, but she wouldn't get as angry. As this went on, I continued to wrap myself in friends at school. Some of the things I began to do were wrong, but in the shadow of wanting attention, my decisions would not be good. Some things were dysfunctional: fibbing, going places I shouldn't have gone, skipping school one time just to go see my old friend who had dropped out to get married and start her family, going to parties, going to friends' houses after school, going just about anywhere to get away from going home. I was running from all of it. Nothing made any sense, but if I acted like Mom, I received her permission to leave, to go see my friends, and that meant getting away from her.

My friction with Mom was escalating. One evening, I was in the kitchen telling her I wanted to go stay with a girlfriend. All at once, she turned and started to hit me hard. Dad happened to be in the living room and came racing into the kitchen. "What the hell are you doing to her?"

Mom proceeded to look at him and say, "She is a goddamn dumbbell, and you know it!" She went to hit me again, and for the first time, Dad raised his hand to her. I saw the fear in her eyes as she looked at Dad with the thought he was going to hit her. He didn't. He just turned and looked at me and said, "Look what you're doing to her!" I didn't realize it, but I was on the floor, leaning against the wall, holding my stomach because it was in so much pain.

I knew I was sick. My stomach hurt all the time. I went to my room. As I sat there, I started to have feelings of leaving this place.

This was the first moment I truly felt out of control. I decided I was going to run away from home. There was a screaming inside of me that no one could hear. I told my girlfriend I was planning to run away. My friend told me I could stay at her house. She was such a dear friend. She and her mother probably saved my life. God knows where I would have gone without them.

My whole family was in the living room watching television. I couldn't clarify why I was doing this. I really think at this point something was going wrong with me. What if I had what my mother had? But I didn't want to think about that. If you are running away from home and you are in a normal state, you pack a few clothes and things, and that would be it. I went back and forth from my bedroom to my car, load after load. I took every piece of clothing I owned. Summer, fall, winter, like I was leaving for the rest of my life. I thought it was unbelievable that I could walk right by the arch hallway without anyone seeing me or wondering what I was doing. I believe I made over forty trips.

I sat down at the little desk in my room and wrote a good-bye letter. It was so mixed up. I basically said no one loves me, life doesn't make sense to me, why was I in it, it would be better for the family if I wasn't around. It was an off-the-wall letter. So much so that my dad ripped it up when he found out I had run away.

I waited until everyone was asleep. I moved my car away from the house so that no one would hear me start it. I crept out of the bed I shared with my sister. Somehow, no one woke up. I drove to my friend's house.

I was wearing my mom's old pink robe when my friend and her mother met me at the door. They were kind and made sure I was okay. They had me go in and lie down. Not a word was spoken about anything. They gave me a couple of aspirin and a hug. They asked no questions. I know my head was in a different world; if someone said anything, I didn't hear it.

In the morning, my friend told me we'd be going to school as usual. I got dressed, and we went. I was riding in my friend's car. I didn't want anyone to see me.

Now think about this: I was going to school where my brother and sister attended. I saw my mom dropping them off. I ducked down in my seat so she wouldn't see me. *What am I doing? What have I done? They are going to kill me.* I wasn't even sure why I did it. At this point, I couldn't think. In my mind, I deserved punishment. It's contradictory to run away but feel guilty as hell for doing it. I tried to avoid parts of the hallway where my brother and sister might be. When they finally saw me in school that morning, they said, "You are in so much trouble!" I really didn't know what or who I was, other than numb.

Somehow I ended up at my uncle and aunt's house that night, and my dad showed up. He had such a pained expression on his face. He looked at me with what seemed like a large question: "Why did you do this?" I wanted to hold him and tell him I was sorry, but I played the emotional victim. I said, "I can't go home right now to Mom. I want to stay here." The next day, they moved me into my grandma's house.

One night, I didn't come home from school until after eleven o'clock. Before I went into the house, I puked my guts out in my grandma's flower bed. I was drunk and didn't feel that I belonged anywhere. When I entered Grandma's house, she was waiting for me. She hit me hard in the head, told me to get to my room, and that I had better never do that again. I wasn't mad at her. I understood I was wrong, and I knew in my heart I wasn't being a good kid. I lay in her spare bed and wondered what was going to happen to me. I welcomed the darkness. It was my best friend. I didn't have to see anyone.

I had broken up with my longtime boyfriend and started dating a new guy. He was fun and exciting. I adored the fact that he was popular in school. I had gotten into the "in crowd."

Being with him and his gang was so welcoming to my soul. I never talked to them about my mom. I loved going over to his house. His mother was so cool and visited with me as if I were an adult. I loved, loved, loved these moments!

Then one day, my mom brought my favorite pie to Grandma's and asked me if I wanted to come home. I had mixed feelings of love and sorrow for doing this to my mom. I wanted to hug her, but that wouldn't happen. My mom was trying to show love for me. My stomach was so mixed up, all I could feel was fear. I told her I would think about it.

I had been having so much pain in my stomach that Dad came and took me to the doctor, who diagnosed me with stomach ulcers. Dad was very upset. I knew he felt badly for me and what I had suffered. I was aware he also endured it, but as a father and husband, he needed to stay strong. My father conveyed a lot of love without saying a word. He had to handle it all. Eventually, I went home.

It was surreal when I went home. I put my things back in my room, but for some reason it wasn't my room anymore. It didn't feel the same. At this point, I wasn't feeling connected to my home.

HONOR ROLL

I had been working hard in school. I was still trying to prove to myself that I wasn't dumb. The last grades came out; they always printed the honor roll kids by grades in the small town newspaper. I read the paper one Thursday evening, and there was my name. I had made the honor roll. It was as though fireworks were shooting off in my head. I felt a weight lifting off me.

"I am not dumb!" I cried in the bathroom so no one could see or hear. I buried my head in a towel and kept saying, "I am not dumb. I am not a dumbbell." I couldn't wait until we all sat down at the supper table. I was going to show my folks the paper. Supper was ready. I couldn't remember feeling this good in a long time. It was a *really* good feeling—not fake, or made up, or acting. We ate, and I told them I made the paper. "I am on the honor roll."

"Boy, that's great!" Dad said.

Mom looked at me, scowling. "You know, they put a lot of kids on the honor roll in the last semester. They feel sorry for all of you, so they just put your name down. You didn't make the real honor roll. You're too stupid." I sat there with the emptiest feeling; I couldn't even cry, I couldn't talk. I got up and went to my room. I put the paper on my shelf for safekeeping and thought, *No, I am not dumb. I will hang on to this feeling. No matter what, I will make it in life.* My heart hurt, and I went to sleep.

It was my senior prom, and I was going to enjoy it! I had a new boyfriend, and Mom let me pick out a beautiful dress. I was set. It was turning out better than I had ever dreamed. All of us were laughing, dancing, and having a wonderful time, looking forward to the party afterward. To top the evening off, the high school had decided to have its first-ever prom king and queen. The ninth through eleventh grades voted on who they wanted. I knew the queen was going to be my friend Kathy. She was so popular. The king was announced—a great classmate named Brett. And then I thought I was hearing things; they said my name. I was stunned. I couldn't move. I was so happy and surprised. Never in my wildest dreams did I expect this. They took our picture sitting under decorations that had been made just for this photo.

After the party, I couldn't wait to tell Dad and Mom the news. When I got home, I knew it was late, but I didn't care. I had to share the news with them. I stopped by their bedroom and told them. Dad kept sleeping.

"You must be drunk or had some drinks. You didn't get prom queen," Mom said.

I went to bed silent. I didn't have a thought in my head. In a few days, the paper came out, and there was my picture.

"I told you. I got prom queen."

"You sure looked pretty. That's really nice," Dad said at the supper table. Mom looked at the picture and never said a word.

Time went by, and now it was the end of my senior year. All my friends were talking about which college they would be attending in the fall. I knew I was smart; I was on the honor roll. I was thinking what college I should attend. Mom was ill again. Dad didn't even talk about the institution anymore. Mom had new symptoms. She would chomp on ice all day long. The chomping was constant, every cube so loud. She continued to look at me the way she always had. I begged my folks to let me go to college.

"You're so dumb. I am not paying money for a dumbbell to go to school and not become anything."

I hated her right then. Nothing was changing in my home. What was I going to do? I could see in my dad's eyes that he was lost as well. The next day, Dad came to school and met with the guidance counselor and me.

"What do you think about Karen going to dog-grooming college in Eugene, Oregon? My sister lives out there."

I couldn't believe what I heard Dad suggesting. I knew I was smarter than that, yet the counselor just sat there looking at me. It was like I had no say in this. I had never even heard of dog-grooming college. The guidance counselor agreed it would be best. He didn't know me, and he never asked me what I wanted. I still felt like I wasn't loved, this time because they had decided to ship me off. I know on some level this didn't make sense—I should *want* to leave my mom and her illness. Yet part of me feared that everything she said about me was true. Maybe I was worthless. Maybe I'd never be able to be on my own. Maybe this would be the only thing I could do.

I wanted to go to college in the fall with all my friends. I wouldn't feel so alone if I had my friends there, too. I didn't want to go somewhere by myself.

It was going to happen whether I wanted it to or not. Professional dog-grooming college was starting June 2 and would continue for three full months, all through the summer. I would miss being with my friends, and then I would come home, and they all would be gone.

I packed my things. The school had studio apartments but said we had to bring our own dishes, towels, and bedding. I started to put four towels into my suitcase. Mom proceeded to take them out, letting me know I couldn't have any of her towels; another show of her hatred for me. I continued to pack, and Mom removed almost everything from the suitcase as I put in it. She wouldn't help me at all. Nor did she talk to me. She just stared at me. My sister watched, too. I have no idea what went through her head.

Dad came into the bedroom. "Your aunt lives in Medford. You know where that is, because we went there to visit a few times. You will stay there, and Aunt Lily will take you to the dog-grooming college in Eugene."

For the first time in my mixed-up world, I believed my father was walking away from me, too. This time, I wasn't running away; I was being shipped away. I wasn't capable of understanding that my dad was trying to give me time away. I had a pit in my stomach. I couldn't feel anything. I just went through the motions of getting my things into the suitcase. I hated this moment. I did not want to go. I wanted to go to college with my friends. I was only seventeen, and had never even been to a big city.

The night before I was supposed to leave, I waited until everyone went to bed. Then I went out to the step in front of the house. I could see the stars there, and I sat and cried. I prayed to

God asking him to help me. I was experiencing the loss of my friends. I knew that when I got back, my friends would be gone. I would miss Dad and my siblings. I wanted to miss Mom, but I couldn't. I thought about my boyfriend. I knew that would end as well. My animals were always my buddies. I wondered if they would miss me. I don't recall how long I sat there, but I stayed until I was tired enough to sleep.

The day came for me to head to Oregon. We weren't going to leave to catch my bus until that evening, so all day, I kept looking at my suitcase, trying to sneak in some shampoo and a few other things. I played with my animals to pass the time.

It was finally time to leave. Dad, Mom, and my sister were taking me to the Greyhound bus station, which was an hour and a half from our home. My brother didn't want to go. We got my bags in the car, and I told Dad I had forgotten something. I wanted to say good-bye to my brother one more time. We had been close, growing up. We fought as siblings do, but we were pals. I went inside, and he was standing in the living room. I hugged him, and for the first time in my life, I realized he loved me, too. He cried with me, and I told him I would miss him. We looked at each other without words, our eyes full of tears. Then I had to leave him.

TO OREGON

I n the car, I cried and held my little sister in the back seat. She held my hand, and tears were running down her face, too. This was the first time I'd felt my sister's love. I think she was getting older and was beginning to understand some things. For some reason at this moment, I wanted to protect her and knew I couldn't.

Finally, my father said, "Do you want me to turn around, or do you want to go?" For a split second, I thought, *Please, say you want me to stay home.* I looked at my mom, and knew I could no longer take her look of not wanting me. I quit crying.

"No, I will go." I just looked out the car window and held my sister's hand. I told myself, *No more tears.* I was scared to death. I felt a chill I couldn't get rid of. Then the strange person inside of me started to come out. *Be glad you're leaving.* A wave of strength came over me. I didn't realize Mom was having another breakdown. I didn't realize I was witnessing a different level of manic depression. I was so engulfed in my inner pain of feeling alone; I couldn't wrap my head around what was happening to her.

We got to the bus station. The people waiting to get on the bus were dressed in simple clothes. I'd already made my first mistake; I was dressed too nicely. I had no idea how to dress for a three-day bus ride. I should have had on jeans, a shirt, and tennis shoes. Instead, I wore pretty pants, a nice top, and low heels. I wish someone would have told me. I felt so out of place.

Dad and Mom followed me onto the bus. I sat down in a seat by the window. I was screaming inside because Mom didn't want to give me a hug good-bye. My father had hugged me before I got on the bus. "I will be on the phone with bus stations and your aunt, and I will know where you are at all times to make sure you get there."

The bus ride would be my first encounter with a world I didn't know yet. It was pitch black outside. I could feel people around me, but I didn't want to look at anyone. As I stared out the window, I saw my dad talking to the bus driver. I knew he would look up at me, and I had to be strong for him. He had been through so much with Mom. I knew in my heart he wouldn't be able to handle it if I cried in front of him now. So when he looked up, I just waved and smiled. My heart broke. As the bus pulled out, I watched my dad, my mom, and my sister get into the car to head home.

I was afraid and so wide awake. I saw others with their eyes shut. There was no way in hell I would shut my eyes! The bus came to a stop in the next town. We had a few minutes to go to the restroom. I needed to pee, but I was too scared I would miss the bus and be left behind. At the first stop, I held my bladder. By the next stop, I had to go no matter what. I didn't realize we were already in a different state.

When I went into the restroom, I had my makeup in my purse. I was putting on some lip gloss when this woman approached me and said, "Give me your lipstick. I want to use it." I was startled and couldn't think, so I just gave it to her. I stood waiting for her to give it back. Instead, she said, "Do you have eye makeup?" I reached into my purse and gave that to her, too. I thought she was a rude person, but being fearful, I wasn't sure what to think.

As I waited, I could see people getting back on the bus. I told her I needed my stuff because I had to go. She looked at me, laughed, and snorted, "Sorry, bitch, this is mine now. You have a problem with that?" She got close to me, but I couldn't speak. She turned and took off. I followed her, thinking she might be getting on my bus and I could tell the bus driver.

Unfortunately, she went to another bus and jumped on. I got on my bus and sat down. I realized at this point I couldn't take anything out of my purse or someone would take it.

On the second day, the bus pulled up to a stop near a desert town. I noticed the ground was all sand, with hardly any trees, just cactus-like plants. I got off the bus for a break. I got back on the bus, and a man sat down next to me. He smelled like booze, and his hair looked greasy and uncombed. I sat close to the side of the seat near the window; there wasn't room to get a toothpick between me and the side of the bus.

It was a long bus ride, and it was starting to get dark. I was thinking of my dad and our family situation, wondering if he really knew where I was. There weren't cell phones at that time, so there was no way to communicate with anyone. I prayed it wasn't far to Medford. I always loved Aunt Lily. I couldn't wait to see her. This was the only secure feeling I had, knowing she would be waiting for me.

Sometime during the night, I heard a whisper in my ear, "Do you want to make it to Oregon?" The man had hold of my hand and said, "You will get me off right now or I will make sure you do not see the rest of this trip." Fear engulfed me. It was a paralyzing fear. Someone was telling me that he was going to kill me. I wanted to scream to the bus driver. The tightness on my arm increased, and I saw he had a knife. It was dark on the bus, but I could see the bus lights' reflection on the blade. He was pointing it right at my side. My mind raced back to when Mom would have hold of me, yelling, "You dumbbell!"

The man started to push the knife into my side so I could feel how sharp it was. I froze.

"Don't say a word, little girl, or it will be your last." He pushed my hand down his pants onto his penis, and I wanted to die. It was happening again. I felt sick as he moved my hand, rubbing it up and down. Such anger was running through me. I thought about trying to break it in half. I wanted to grab it harder and tear it off his body.

The feeling of self-preservation I had when Mom hit me came over me. *Don't feel a thing. Do as he says. Don't feel a thing.* I went into the zone I had known so well growing up.

My mind could take me away, staying in a robot state with no feelings at all.

He must have finished, as I realized my hand was back on my lap, not being held. I reached down with my other hand and clasped my hands together tightly. There wasn't any feeling in my used hand. It was as if it wasn't attached to me. The smell of his cum was making me sick to my stomach. I wanted the bus to stop. I wanted to scream, but I was terrified he would kill me. I cried quietly, and my body was cold. It was still dark outside, so no one could see my face.

Finally, we were pulling into a town. The bus stopped. The man got up to leave. When he looked back at me, it was as though he threatened me without saying a word. I sat still. I couldn't get up. I was terrified he might be outside waiting for me.

As everyone was coming back onto the bus, a new lady came by and asked if she could sit by me. I am sure I looked like a ghost. I said, "Please, that would be great." I couldn't say anything else. I didn't want to talk with anyone. I wanted to go home. I wanted off the bus. I wondered how they could put me on this bus. No one cared. I was retreating inside myself again, where no one else was allowed.

I was nervous most of the time, and I'm not proud of it, but I started to smoke cigarettes. Every time I got off the bus, I smoked. It was becoming a crutch, one I would have for a while. I knew I had to hide my smoking from my aunt. I couldn't tell people how nervous I was. Trusting people became a roadblock for me. I was a lost soul traversing through life.

Finally, it was daylight, and the bus came to a stop. I heard the driver say, "Medford, Oregon." I looked out the window, and there was my aunt. I stepped off the bus and hugged her. She hugged me back.

"It is so good to see you, Karen."

She loved me. It was the sentiment I needed. I wasn't sure if I was hugging her or just hugging to feel someone safe.

As we drove off, I thought about telling my aunt about the incident on the bus ride, but I knew it would get back to Mom, and she would just tell me once again how dumb I'd been. She'd blame me. It would be my fault. She would say I was a slut and remind me more than once not to bring a papoose home with me.

I didn't know whether Dad would believe me, so I pushed the event deep within my heart, where no one else would see it. I knew how to be alone with my secrets.

In a way, I was scared to stay at my aunt's home. I loved her, and she was always laughing and smiling, but I didn't know her very well. I didn't think she knew about my family. I wondered if she knew my "normal." Did her brother, my dad, tell her anything? I stayed quiet; I didn't have much to say. I noticed my aunt was pretty "with it" for a middle-aged lady. I enjoyed the peace in her house. Her normal was certainly different from mine. She enjoyed showing me all her canned jars of pickles. I stayed for a couple of days. I opened the small window in the shower and smoked. I'm sure my aunt knew, but she never said a word.

It was time to leave for Eugene. Aunt Lily talked with me all the way. I listened to every word. I loved the stories she shared about her life in Oregon. I learned her thoughts about my situation. She couldn't believe her brother would let me stay by myself in a large city, with only a bike to ride back and forth to school.

My aunt and I pulled into the studio apartments, found mine, and went in. It was furnished with a vinyl couch, a table, and two chairs. I looked at my aunt, wanting to cry, but didn't say a thing. "Well," she said, "let's go shopping."

Dad had sent her money, so we went and bought towels, some disposable plates, and a bike to ride to school. We went back to my apartment, which was basically a room.

I noticed there was a door with a lock on it in the back. I opened it, and we walked into a very large kitchen. A painted-up old lady was sitting there, in the middle of the day, wearing a red see-through nightgown.

"We all share this kitchen."

God, I wanted to run! I just stared at her. I couldn't help but notice one of her breasts was exposed. Then she said, "You might come out here and see men sleeping on the floor. They come to visit me." I couldn't figure out what she meant.

Aunt Lily said, "Nice to meet you," and we went back into my room. She locked the door, sat me down, and said, "I need to educate you on some things, my dear, and you need to listen."

I didn't know what to say, but replied, "How do I cook? I don't have any pans or anything. I don't know where the grocery store is. What do I do with just a bike?" I wanted so much to say, "I want to go home," but, I thought, *Go home to what?*

Once again, I kept my sadness to myself. *Remember you're a dumbbell,* the words kept repeating in my head.

"We'll get you a microwave, and you have a small fridge in here, so you will be okay." We went and she found a grocery store a few blocks away. "You might have to go every other night; you can only handle one bag on your bike." She took good care of me, I was glad she was going to stay for a couple of days.

She got my phone hooked up and then said, "Let's see if your dad is home." I hadn't talked with my family in over a week. I listened to them talk. My aunt had no problem scolding my dad for not sending me with towels. She let Dad know we bought everything I needed, including an all-in-one alarm clock / radio. She said, "I am going to drive her on the route, so she knows how to get to the dog-grooming college and back." She handed the phone to me. I heard Dad's voice, and I wanted so badly to cry, but I told him I was fine and it looked okay here.

I was lying. I had never seen a city like this, and I wasn't used to anything resembling it. We made small talk, and then we said good-bye. I wondered if anyone noticed that Mom didn't talk with me, nor did she ask to.

My aunt went on to explain to me what a hooker was, and that cleared up the painted old woman. I could see the concern in her eyes. Once again, she reminded me to stay out of the shared kitchen. She could tell I was living in a semi-rough part of the city, but it was the area closest to the school. My college for the next three months was about three miles away, making it six miles to bike each day. I thought it would be good for me. My aunt proceeded to tell me not to go out when it was dark. That's when I noticed the big front window to my apartment had bars over it, so no one could break in. The door wasn't wood; it was heavy metal. I promised Aunt Lily I would be careful.

I wondered how I would spend my evenings without a television. My aunt got ready to leave. She told me to jump on a bus to come see her over the Fourth of July. I agreed, but just saying the word *bus* made me feel sick.

I set my alarm clock for the first day of school. I was scared, and I had no one. I just sat on the old vinyl couch and smoked.

The first day I biked to school, guys yelled and whistled at me from their cars. I pedaled faster, not looking at anyone. I walked in and found that my instructor was a lady. She owned the college. Her name was Ms. Mavis.

"You must be my girl from Nebraska."

I liked her instantly. She told me to bring my bike inside and keep it in the back, or it wouldn't be there when school was over.

Needless to say, my guard was up, but I made friends in class. I realized I would have to learn to groom over three hundred breeds. I had to learn their anatomy, bones and all. This was more than a grooming place; it was a college with a test every Friday.

All at once, I realized I was not a dumbbell. No one here knew anything about me, my family, or my home. I could show them how smart I was. I threw myself into school, learning everything and working very hard. I was getting straight As on my tests. I was grooming and learning the various clipper blades, the art of what national dog groomers do. I learned about professional dog shows and how groomers make the dogs look so good.

Every day, I was progressing in this program. I shut out my past; I blocked my mind from all of it. These people didn't know my mom, so I planned to make friends and excel at school.

My love for animals was going to save me again.

At night, I called friends, and my dad complained about the phone bill he had to pay, but I didn't have a TV. I just sat on the vinyl couch, smoked, and talked to my friends for hours each evening to pass the time. I realized I was starting to lose my friends. They didn't have much to say and were getting too busy to be on the phone.

Things were changing at home; life was moving on without me. My boyfriend started dating other girls. I was crushed. All I had were my few new friends at college and my love of working with dogs every day.

It was starting to dawn on me that it had been over a month and Mom had never called me. It seemed as if I never existed to her. I wondered if she even thought about me.

At the dog school, Ms. Mavis sometimes looked at me like she could tell I was a lost soul. She smiled at me a lot and told me I was a wonderful treat to have in class. I know now that angels come in all forms. God gave me an angel to be there for me, so I wouldn't feel so alone. Mavis was my angel.

The other girls in the college were older than I was and invited me to their places on the weekends. They all lived locally; I was the only one from out of state. It turned out to be a welcome distraction from what was going on at home. I guess my dad knew what I needed after all.

I was learning about city life. One day, while riding my bike with my bag of groceries, this lady who was not much older than I was came right up to me in the grocery store parking lot.

"I have to ask you, because I see you ride your bike past my house a lot, and you can hardly carry your bag and purse, could you use some help?"

I spilled my guts and told her I lived alone and that all I had was a bike. I thank God to this day that she wasn't a bad person. She wasn't trying to hurt me or steal something from me. Her name was Mary, and she turned out to be a very nice lady. She was young and attended the normal college in Eugene. She and her boyfriend, who was also in college, lived together in a rental house nearby. Long story short, she said she would come by every Saturday to pick me up and give me a ride to the store and back. That way, I could get a week's worth of groceries all at once. I asked her why she wanted to do this for me.

She just said, "You seem like a nice girl who could use a friend." She remained my friend all summer. Mary invited me over many evenings for supper and to hang out with them. It was wonderful to be with them because they played great music, and we laughed a lot. They told me all about the city.

This was my first time seeing a white woman with a black man. *Wow*, I thought, *we are behind the times at home.* I realized I had no clue what the world was really like. I was absorbing it all, but I still didn't share anything about my mom. I buried it and let my new friends think my life was grand.

Nights were challenging for me. I was scared, lonely, and lost. I felt like a stick person walking around a cement city.

I did go to my aunt's on the Fourth of July. My uncle Leo and their daughter, Shirley, was also there. Shirley was married. They had just had their second baby girl. I offered to babysit for her. She told me she and Mike had never had a date night without their kids, so they were so happy to get one. It felt good to feel like I belonged to their family. I went back to Eugene hating leaving my relatives. I wouldn't see them again on this trip.

One morning at school, Ms. Mavis said, "I want to talk with you. We haven't had a student graduate from this college with recommendations in five years. You have surpassed all the records here at our school."

I couldn't believe what I was hearing. "You mean I groomed at the highest level, and scored highest on all the paper tests, too?"

She said, "You nailed everything."

I hugged her, thanking her for the kind words.

She said, "You're the one who put in all of the effort and accomplished it. Be proud."

For many years, I would not know the secret she was keeping. I had been offered a position grooming dogs for a world-renowned breeder and owner. He had been a winner at professional dog shows all over the world. They needed a professional groomer. It would have been the chance of a lifetime. But I was only seventeen and wouldn't turn eighteen for a month. Ms. Mavis had told my father about the offer, and he told her not to say anything to me. He said I was too young and needed to come home. Later in life, I found out about the offer and wondered what my life could have been. Had I known, I'd have gone.

Of course, having no idea, I was excited to call Dad to say I was ready to come home. I'd graduated early because of my excellent grades. I could hear the excitement in his voice. "I will send out John, our hired man, and your brother. Grandma can ride along, too. It will be a treat for all of them." I thought, *I can see my grandma needing a vacation, but my brother, wow, he must miss me!*

The excitement was overwhelming. I couldn't wait to see them and return home.

Saying good-bye to the people who had helped me forget about my home for three months was difficult. I'd grown to love them. They had no idea what a gift they were.

Ms. Mavis threw a good-bye party for me. "If you ever need me, just give me a call."

I promised I would. On the way home, riding in the truck, I was thinking, *What's it going to be like for Mom and me?* She hadn't called or talked to me in three months. I was wondering if she hated me that much. Once home, I couldn't wait to hug my dad, and maybe even Mom, if she would. My hopes were that Mom would be better and all would be good.

While I was in Eugene, a gal cut my hair and gave me a perm. She was one of the students, but loved working on ladies more than dogs. I liked my new hairdo, the cut being a new style we found in a magazine. It hung on my shoulders with soft curls that seemed to bounce when I walked. We pulled in the driveway, and my sister came running up to the pickup with Mom right behind her. I looked at Mom before the door opened. She looked grouchy. My brother opened the door. I was in the middle, and Mom looked at me.

"Hi, Mom."

"What the hell have you done to your hair?"

It was like the whole world disappeared. I instantly felt numb, fear set in, and I wondered if she was going to hit me. My sister just looked at me, not knowing what to say.

The rolling pit and nervous feeling returned to my stomach. The feeling that had gone away for a few months was back. *Oh, God, I have to feel this way again!* My eyes filled with tears, and the hurt was deep.

I asked my brother, "Where is my car? Are the keys in it?" I ran to my car and drove down the lane as fast as I could to reach the field where Dad was putting up hay. Dirt rolled from my tires. Then I saw him. I stopped. I don't even know if I shut off the car. I ran to him. He jumped off the tractor and gave me the biggest hug. I loved my dad. I realized at that moment, it had always been Dad and me who were the victims of Mom's illness. We hung in there together, and that is, and was, the strength we carried deep within ourselves. I was thankful Dad had given me a break that summer. I was smart enough to know that he was trying to give me a skill so I would be able to leave and be okay on my own. It's hard to say, but I know Dad needed me to leave, because watching Mom's and my interactions tore him up.

In the house, I knew what was coming. Mom wasn't any better than when I'd left. I think Dad was just tolerating Mom now, putting up with her crazy statements. He had gotten used to them. We all had. Mom kept reminding me of my dumbbell status because I let my friend curl my hair. I was tired and wanted to sleep in my own bed, so I headed down the hall. I lay there thinking of my summer and how, for a moment in time, I was happy. I wasn't stupid. I knew it wouldn't be long, and I would need to leave again. I could tell our home was better without me in it.

It took me a while to realize many of my things from my bedroom were gone. I couldn't find my class yearbook albums, where all my friends had written notes to me. I looked all around for the ribbons I had won at the Saddle Club. Before I left, I probably had fifty or more ribbons hanging on my vanity. I had memories that had been pinned up on the bulletin board, and now those were gone, too. Where the heck were my things? Did Mom put everything in a box? It reinforced my sense that Mom didn't want me there.

It had been all thrown away. For the first time, I yelled at my mom. "Where are my things? All my things from growing up? From high school? All my memories?" She told me they had cleaned up. As I looked over the room, it was all my sister's now. It was as though I had never lived there. I was only gone three months. I knew from my girlfriends that their parents had put all their things into boxes, ready to take with them someday. Mine had been burned in a garbage barrel; I could never get them back. I had nothing to show for my life up to this point. She left me only one thing: a miniature cardboard picture of me playing volleyball. I still don't know why that was left. I keep it out now, for the sake of all the memories of my childhood that were lost forever.

In her crazed capacity, who knows why she would leave things. It might have been simply because of the colors I had on.

I wish she would have hit me or called me names instead of burning my things. I was completely empty. I went for a long walk down the lane to the river and watched the water race past. I asked God what I was supposed to be or do. I was a lost soul with no direction.

I knew my dad loved me, but he couldn't protect me from it all. The raging voice came from inside of Mom. I wasn't worth anything to her. That evening, I looked at my dad. He was quiet; he just didn't have the humor or the desire to visit anymore. I still wonder what was in his mind when he was quiet; maybe he was lost, too.

Mom called me an old soul. Maybe she was right. I was feeling like I had lived a lifetime already. After all my things were gone, I knew I was no longer wanted. I figured Mom would always be this way and that she'd always feel this way about me. I was a misfit toy.

The next morning, Dad and I started to look in the paper for jobs. I couldn't believe I was looking for dog-groomer positions. I really wanted to be something more than that—a dream I had to bury. Dad said, "Lo and behold, here is an ad for a dog groomer. They need help at a pet store in Kearney. It's about seventy-three miles away. Not bad." Dad and Mom actually knew the couple who owned the store. At one point, they had been neighbors in the little town where we used to live. One phone call from Dad, and I had an interview.

The next day, we drove to Kearney. Dad said, "This will be good for you. To get started, anyway." I wanted to throw up. I kept thinking, *I am not stupid. I am smarter than you think.* I had to keep saying this because I couldn't believe what was happening.

We met Kathy. The way she looked at me gave me an incredibly spooky feeling. The store looked like a long, dark, hollow warehouse. Then she said she would only pay forty dollars per week. I couldn't believe my ears. I learned in dog grooming college what we should get paid. I couldn't afford an apartment on that. Dad said, "Well, she can't live here and pay bills on that." Kathy said, "She can move into one of my extra bedrooms. Our girls are raised, so she can have her own bedroom and bath." I didn't feel I had any say. I had to do it.

The facility was terrible for grooming dogs. She had me grooming on a card table without the equipment I needed. Nothing but dull scissors and an old bathtub for bathing the dogs. I had to bring my own professional dog dryer. There was carpet on the floor so all the dog hair had to be vacuumed. It was a filthy hole in which to groom dogs. She wouldn't purchase blades for my clippers, yet expected me to do good work with dull ones. I couldn't use them because they hurt the dogs, pulling their hair. I tried my best with just my pair of scissors. Then she criticized my work. Kathy was showing her true colors. I had graduated from a top grooming college in Oregon with the highest recommendation, but she called my dad and said I wasn't good enough. This set my mom off.

"Good thing we didn't waste money on her with college."

I knew Kathy was lying and not telling Dad what was really going on here. I didn't know what her issues were, but it was mental abuse. I knew this woman should be turned in. She sold puppies from a small cage where they couldn't even move. I wished I could have saved them by taking them all home with me.

I truly disliked Kathy. After midnight, she made me go get fish from the train station delivery to restock the aquariums. She enjoyed being abusive. I couldn't believe it. I left home, and I still couldn't get away from mental abuse.

I finally called Dad and said, "I can't groom without tools. She won't order me what I need to make the dogs look good." Then I realized there was a purpose for her meanness. She had made a deal with Dad that she would keep me on if I did more work for the same pay. Emotionally, I couldn't take it. She was starting to stare at me like my mom did. I couldn't even play the mental game with her.

I was getting fearful something was going wrong inside of me. I was getting sick. I didn't know what to do. I was regressing; I wasn't happy. I couldn't smile. Was this how Mom felt when she was ill? Did I have what she had? Finally, it came to a raging end. Kathy had no idea I had already seen it all. *Abuse me all you want, bitch, I am used to it.*

After work, I had nowhere to go. I stayed at the pet store cleaning up until late. I didn't want to go to her house, to just lie there in my little room with no TV. I felt I was going to go crazy in the head like Mom. Driving back to her house, I wanted to just keep driving and never stop. As I lay on the bed in this small room with nothing to do, I couldn't help but feel that I was in a padded room with the door locked and no one was letting me free of this mental abuse. I hated my life at this moment. It seemed to me that no one wanted me around.

It was a Friday, and I wasn't feeling well. I decided to drive back to see my folks. I got a few miles out of town and realized I had forgotten my purse, so I had to go back. The door was locked, but I had my key, so I let myself in. I had to go past the living room to get to my room, and there she was, in sexy red lingerie. I had no idea who the gentleman was, but it wasn't her husband. I said, "Excuse me," and raced to my room, grabbed my bag, and left quickly. I don't know where they went, but I hurried to my car and left.

On the way home from Kearney, I had to stop my car several times and open the car door to puke my guts out. I didn't realize I was having an appendix attack. I drove straight to the doctor's office and told them what I was feeling. Within minutes, Dad came racing into the lobby, and they told us I had to have an emergency appendectomy. When I woke up, Dad was sitting by me in the hospital. I looked around. I never said a word about Mom not being there.

When I was home healing, I shared with Dad what I had seen. I told him we needed to start looking for another job, because I couldn't stay with this woman. Mom just looked at me and said nothing. I kept thinking, *Isn't there going to be a day that you come back to me and love me? Or will you hate me my whole life?* I never felt like it was home for me now or that it would ever be again.

I had taken a week to heal, then headed back to Kathy's. I walked in, and she and her husband were there. They said they were glad I was feeling better. I went straight to my room. I had a few boxes, so I started packing some of my belongings.

I went to work the next day and worked all day until suppertime. I went home expecting to eat with them. Kathy said they had already eaten, but there was spaghetti in the kitchen. I went in, and the pan was empty. There was no food for me. She was teaching me a lesson, "Catch me at home with another man, and you'd better shut up or you don't eat."

I walked back in, and her husband asked, "Aren't you going to eat?" I told him I wasn't hungry. I had to get out of this situation. Out of fear, I couldn't say anything. I was truly scared to death of her.

Angels came again to my rescue. Dad called me the next day and said there was a job fifty miles from where I was. It was at an animal hospital with four veterinarians. They wanted someone available to groom dogs and be a vet assistant. My dad always had my back and did watch out for me the best he could. I called and set the interview up for Saturday. I drove down, landed the job, and told one of the doctors about Kathy. I wasn't going to give two weeks' notice.

I had saved some money. I stopped at an old hotel that rented apartments and signed up for one starting the next day. I didn't have much, just some clothes and a small stereo. I called my dad and told him I was moving myself to this new job. I loaded my things and told Kathy I quit. I thought about telling her husband what I had seen, but I was scared of what she might do. Still feeling like a loner, I knew I had to keep going. There wasn't even a thought I could go home.

What had all of this done to me? I was running again, but I was protecting myself the best I could. I couldn't bear any kind of abuse anymore. If I had known then what I know now, I would have asked for help for my own mental status.

I was hoping this move would change my life. Getting away from home hadn't helped. The abuse follows the child. The mental buildup within dictates how a person feels about herself and that, in turn, influences what type of person will be drawn to her.

At this point in my life, I still didn't know who I was. I didn't know what I loved or what I wanted to do. I was directionless. I was moving through life with no goal, and no one to talk to about it.

All my belongings fit into my car. I packed and drove away from Kathy's as fast as I could.

I drove into the new town and unloaded my things into this strange hotel room. When I opened the door, I had to tilt my head back to see the ceiling. The marble floor was made up of one-inch black-and-white squares. It reminded me of the old courthouse I had gone into with Dad. The smell was the same, too, like an opened Pine-Sol bottle. The room was cold and dark. It was disconcerting. The bed pulled down from the wall. It was the only piece of furniture there was. The only light in the room came from a floor lamp. I was glad I had a job to go to, because I hated this place. It was nothing I wanted to come home to. The only good thing was that my room was right on top of the police station, so in a strange way, I felt safe.

When I started my new job, all the staff and bosses were nice, except for one doctor. It took me a while to win him over. I felt he didn't like having a woman working around all the guys. He seemed old-fashioned, like he thought it was supposed to be a man's world. Eventually, he discovered that I worked hard and didn't complain. I was quiet, and I wasn't there to flirt with anyone. The last thing I needed was more drama in my life.

I was enjoying my veterinary assistant job. I became good friends with the secretary. She had been there for years. I think she knew more than anybody. Life was going well. I had been taking care of this little lost dog no one was claiming. They said I could adopt her if I wanted to. I jumped at the chance to have a dog of my own, a new little friend, a companion. I named her Misty.

I had no idea why I accepted whatever people said or did to me. I didn't realize my struggle wasn't over. While working at the vet clinic, I was introduced to a young man my age. I thought he was good looking, but that was about it. We started to date, and I could tell he had an incredible ego.

At first I was feeling good because someone wanted to be around me. I was a bit nervous, because up until then, boyfriends had just wanted to be around me for their own needs, which often meant sex, with no serious feelings for me at all. I had not found someone who wanted to be with me because he cared about me.

Meanwhile, I really was learning a lot about veterinarian work and how to treat animals. It took some of the doctors a while to realize I was driven, was hardworking, and would do anything they asked of me at work. Some things were challenging, but being with animals again was so comforting. I loved knowing that every morning I would wake up, go to work, and find the dogs and indoor animals all waiting eagerly to be fed. They were always excited to see me. Their energy was therapeutic.

My new boyfriend and I became more serious. We had fun, but I didn't feel excited to be with him. Dating him was something I did because I was getting attention. As time went on, he was getting more comfortable around me. I don't know if I thought about it getting more serious yet or not.

I made a trip to see my family. I loved seeing everyone, and I accepted the way Mom treated me, as long as I could be on the farm and see my dad, siblings, and animals. I still struggled to feel like this was my home, but I had to come back once in a while because deep down, I still felt or prayed that I belonged somewhere.

I returned to Central City and saw my boyfriend's truck at the Dairy Queen. I decided to stop to say hi and get a Diet Coke. As I walked in, I saw he was sitting with his friends, barely fifteen feet away from me. I was at the counter ordering my drink. He would not look at me or greet me in front of his friends. The feeling of betrayal was instant, the rejection overwhelming. Hate entered my body. I took my Coke and went home to my apartment. I thought I should kick him to the curb for being such a jackass. I couldn't believe how quickly anger poured out of me at this painful moment.

Right at this time, he drove up, all cocky, walking into my apartment. I wanted to scream and let him have it. I didn't want to tolerate this emotional abuse. I turned and continued to put my clothes away. I couldn't believe I didn't scream at him to get out. Again, the fear of being alone had won over.

I heard him say, "Let's go out and see my friends." As we were driving out there, I didn't talk much. There were a lot of questions running through my head.

We all went out for supper that evening. They were a nice couple. On the way home, I was telling a funny story about something that happened at work. I hadn't realized it, but my voice was getting louder as I told my story. All of a sudden, something hit me on the back of my head. I instantly went quiet. He'd hit me hard. I felt the strike reverberate all through my body, just as I had all my life. Then he said, "You are talking too loud."

Why didn't I tell him to go to hell and be done with him? I just took it. I thought of my dear friend Becky, sitting up front; she was quiet. They had to have known he did something, because I just went quiet in the middle of a sentence.

I would come to learn later in my life that Becky was abused by her husband; she understood more than I knew. We went on more dates. I never felt anything for him. To me, he was just a companion so that I wouldn't have to be alone. We were out with his friends, and he said for a joke, "Let's get married before my buddy here does." I said, "Yes." There wasn't any romantic gesture or hug. It was as if we were talking about some food we had just eaten. In the back of my mind, I thought, *Don't do it!* But I needed to belong somewhere, and this was one way.

When I told my dad I was getting married, it's like he knew.

"Can't you wait awhile? It's pretty soon into your relationship. Maybe you should give it more time."

I should have listened, but I chose not to. My fear of being alone, and sense of still not being good enough, pushed me to hang on. I felt I had to make my own home, because I didn't have one anymore. I got caught up in the idea of getting married and making a home, and I thought about that instead of thinking about the person who was often unkind to me. Plans were set.

I noticed my mom was in a new-but-calm state of mind. Mom wasn't mean to me. She was just quiet. I liked this in her. I was glad she was being silent for now. This time was somewhat different. I don't know if it's because she had been mentally ill for so long, or because the brain changes with this disease. Anyway, she helped me plan my wedding day. Whoever this Mom was, I had her back for now.

We went together to try on wedding dresses and found one she liked. We had a bridal shower, and she was spot-on that day. I could not have asked for a better mom. I was drawn to her at that moment. I was still nervous inside—a feeling I couldn't shake—but I was proud of her, and loved her so much right then.

Before I knew it, the day of my wedding arrived. My mother was incredible, and I found myself wishing that the two of us could go away somewhere together and just be. I can't remember her ever being so kind to me before or ever looking at me with such love in her eyes. I was eighteen and felt I was finally getting my mother back.

My mother and I talked when I was preparing for the ceremony. I knew how smart she was, but it was like she could read me. It was as if she knew I didn't want to get married. Mom said, "You don't have to go through with this. I will explain to your father." I looked at her and didn't know how to tell her I wasn't strong enough to handle the embarrassment and humiliation. I wanted to tell her the truth. I wanted to run away from this man and his abusive attitude. I couldn't get the words to come. She touched my veil, and it was like a fairy-tale moment. She hugged me and kissed my cheek. I looked in her eyes as tears built in mine.

I didn't know how I could explain canceling the wedding to the man I was seconds from marrying. I was sure he would lose his temper. I was marrying him just to have a home of my own. I couldn't tell 150 people to go home because I didn't want to get married. The screaming in my head was telling me, *Don't do this!* I was scared of people making fun of me again, so I just went ahead with it.

I thought of the boyfriend I'd had my senior year of high school. I trusted him more than I trusted the man I was about to marry. Why couldn't I run?

My weakness, my hell, my decision. I wasn't well in my heart and mind.

The abuse started on the honeymoon. He ignored me and didn't want to be physical. I just stayed with it. The abuse continued, and I found him to be unfaithful. Then I discovered he preferred dirty magazines to being with me. I was enraged. I boxed up all his magazines and burned them in the trash barrel outside. It felt wonderful! He was pissed off, but it didn't change anything. The verbal abuse continued as though it was his right. I didn't care about the marriage or even saying I was married anymore. Once again, I was lost, unloved, and full of mental anguish. I believed I was ugly and not good enough. The feelings I had for him now joined those I'd felt for Mom. I found myself finding places to go to avoid being near him. I still had my wonderful vet assistant job in town. That was my salvation.

He stopped coming home right after work. Neither of us seemed to be able to say, "This is a joke! Let's end this nightmare." When I wasn't working, I would take the dogs and walk for hours in the pasture behind our farmhouse. It was just me and the dogs, which in some way felt perfect.

One day, our neighbors invited us over for supper. They had a little boy with special needs. He was the sweetest little guy. I loved playing with him and getting his special hugs. I went into the kitchen to help his mom set the table, when she put her hand on my arm ever so gently and asked if I was okay.

I looked into her warm face and said, "No, not really. Why?"

"I am concerned for you, your husband is out there talking with mine, and he only refers to you as a bitch." I looked down at the table, utterly embarrassed. Then I was pissed off. I could feel my mind wanting to snap. I didn't want her to see how much anger I had inside. I turned and gave her a hug, thanked her for letting me know, and then asked her if it would be okay if I left. "Maybe your husband can give him a ride home. I need to leave."

I walked past both of them as I went to get into the pickup to go home.

"Where the hell are you going?"

I couldn't help myself. I turned toward him, and everything around me seem to blur except for his face. "Home, bitch!" I had so much rage inside when I left their driveway, I pressed my foot to the floorboard. I am sure anyone for miles could see the cloud of dirt hurling behind me. Later, I heard the door slam as he came into the house. Neither of us said a word. It was an ice-cold air of silence.

Once again, the feeling of abandonment flooded my thoughts. I still didn't know who I was or that I should try to discover myself. Instead, I desperately wanted the void filled. I wanted something to call my own. I stayed in the relationship and coexisted, feeling somewhat trapped.

The feeling of not being able to leave seemed to overtake me. I wondered how I could make my life better. There was only one thing I could do to fix my void. I decided I wanted a baby.

I got my wish and was thrilled. Life was wonderful. I had someone to call my own. I was loving the attention everyone was giving me and my precious baby. It didn't matter whether or not I was getting attention from my husband. I had a baby who needed me and *me alone*. My dad and mom loved our new addition, and I loved that Grandma Ella was still alive to meet my little girl. This, I believed, would be enough in my life.

It wasn't long before another kind of mistreatment came my way. I could tell something was wrong, but couldn't figure out why my husband paid zero attention to me. We had no conversations, and when he did come home, he just turned on the television. It didn't take rocket science to know he was getting "serviced" somewhere else.

The insult took a different turn. Yelling kicked in, but I was used to that, so I just took it. I was busy raising my daughter and didn't really care what he did.

My father offered my husband a job on the farm as a hired hand. I loved my father so much for doing this. I missed my family. I knew he could use my help with Mom. I needed his support more than he knew. I felt guilty for not telling him about my husband's temper. For some reason, I needed to go home.

I had been away from home for a couple of years now, and going home was a big deal for me. How would it go with my mom now that I was also a mom? I was nervous, but I also knew I would help Dad and my mother with anything. I wondered in the back of my mind if I came home to help care for Mom.

My mother had gone to some new doctors, and they had changed her treatment. They had her taking roughly twelve different pills per day. I noticed she wasn't mean anymore; she was just quiet. She still drank her beer, and when combined with the pills, she still slept a lot. Dad was busy on the farm, just as he always had been. It was like time stood still, waiting for my return.

My husband had a bad temper. It wasn't long before he started to yell and talk down to my dad. In the middle of all this, I had another baby, a son. He was the light of our eyes. Now I had two wonderful children to call my own.

I still had no feelings for my husband. I recall when Mom put me down, yelling and hitting me. I'd stopped caring and stopped feeling anything. The same behavior followed me into my marriage. The only thing I knew was love for my children.

I made my whole world about them. I always was concerned about their learning. At lunchtime, I'd let them watch *Sesame Street*. That was a daily event. I took time sitting with them, playing. I made a conscious decision that I would make sure they never felt dumb. I never wanted them to feel they didn't get enough hugs. I wanted them to always feel loved. Mom walked over almost every afternoon to play with the kids. Then she'd lie down on my couch for her afternoon nap. My sister would stop by from time to time and play with the kids, too. She was off going to college. I wanted so much to tell her, "You're living my dream."

One day, out of the blue, Mom said, "You're really a good mom." Then she went into the kids' room and sat down on one of their little chairs and said, "Let's have a tea party." I don't know how long I stood in the doorway watching her play with my children. I was trying to feel the love she was giving them. They were experiencing a loving grandma from the very woman whose love I'd missed. The repercussions of not having support and guidance, of not being educated about what was happening in the home, led to a lifetime of yearning for the parent I never had.

My folks were celebrating their twenty-fifth wedding anniversary. I hosted the party at my home, inviting every friend and relative. Everyone was laughing and talking. Dad came up to me and said, "Isn't it wonderful Mom is doing incredibly well today?" Dad was so proud and thankful that he got this one special gift that day . . . the lucidity of his wife, his soul mate, the love of his life, Evelyn. I looked at them, Mom in her long, beautiful lavender dress, and Dad in his gray suit and tie. It was almost like years were wiped off their faces. A youthful glow had returned. I believe the angels gave them that day as if nothing had ever happened.

Life moved on, as it does. My sister got married. My brother was married. It was all good. Months went by with only a few moments of Mom slipping into negative thoughts and words; it was nothing compared to what we were all used to. Mom's mental illness had seemed to go into remission. I don't believe my siblings had the same life with Mom that I did. It seemed like I had been singled out. Now as an adult and mother, I know Dad and I took the most blows. I am sure my siblings' memories of our young lives, of what it was like to grow up with our mother, are somewhat different from my own. I know they had a softer experience with our mother, and I will always be grateful for that.

Life looked like it was taking a toll on my father, and I wondered how I could have dragged Dad into a relationship with another abusive person. Mom was getting mental episodes once again. My husband insulted my father and treated the machinery like hell. He would take Dad's pickup and spin the tires out in our fields when he got mad at my dad. He had a problem agreeing with my dad's ways of running the farm. In all my life, Dad had never disliked someone without good reason. My father was a wonderful man; people would visit with him about their ideas, and he would talk things through with them. My husband was not a good communicator. He was stubborn and thought things should be his way or the highway. I was getting tired of his bullshit, and I didn't like being in the same house with him. This went on for years, and I still couldn't get the strength to end the marriage.

I had my children, who consumed my world. I was starting to cook lunch for Dad and my husband so Mom wouldn't have to. I helped on the farm, and did some babysitting, and groomed people's dogs on my back porch.

The abuse was getting worse. One day, we were working sick calves, and my husband took out his anger on a small calf that was ill with pneumonia and couldn't move fast. He hit it with a pipe right on the head in the temple area. It dropped dead instantly. None of us could believe the malice. Dad yelled at my husband, saying, "Look what you did!" Then he looked straight at me. "We've got to get him out of here." I looked into my father's face and saw the pain and hurt my so-called husband was causing.

I looked at my father and wanted to say, "You have no idea what I have been through. It's way overdue for him to leave." I turned and started walking to my house. I could feel the heat on my face from the anger that was building inside my body. I couldn't bear to see someone hurt an animal.

In my new role, caretaking for my mom, cooking for Dad and whoever else was about, tending the garden, and helping with all the other farm chores, I was getting protective. For the first time in my life, I made a move.

I told my husband to get out. We were divorcing. He wasn't going to hurt us anymore. He wasn't going to enjoy being a part of the wonderful accomplishments of my father's hard work. I found out something about myself on this journey: *no one* hurts my dad. Strength was starting to grow inside of me.

My mother was beginning to let me care for her, and my dad was finding out that I was still there for him. When I came home from filing for divorce, my folks were watching the kids. Everyone was quiet, as if there had been a funeral. The wonderful thing about my family was that they never celebrated anything that was painful for anyone. Even though they were glad he was gone, they expressed sadness for the situation. I realized then that I had come home to raise my family and be there for Mom. I returned home to take care of the woman who had been ill for most of her life and hurt me for most of mine.

MY NEW ROLE

I took on my new role as a single parent. I wasn't getting much financial assistance from my ex-husband, so to make ends meet, I needed two jobs. I pursued more education so I could be a nurse's aide, and I also worked as a flag person on a construction job. My family stepped up to help me. My sister-in-law watched the kids so I could work. I was ever so grateful! I helped my dad and brother when needed. My brother had come home from college to work the farm with Dad. My sister and her family lived on a ranch and life was in place now.

Mom was taking all ten or more pills that the doctor prescribed for her, and she still drank beer. Her routine didn't change. She slept most of the day. The combination of all this was sinking her into a dark world. She didn't talk much anymore, and we all got used to her being that way. She quit going to church functions. It was as if she was giving up on living any kind of life with her family.

I loved my grandmother Ella very much. As a young mother myself, I finally fully appreciated how strong she'd been, to know her daughter had mental issues and to have to watch all those painful moments. She always stood by Mom's side, no matter what happened. She talked about my grandpa and how much she missed him. She looked forward to being with him again someday.

One day, she went into the hospital not feeling well. I visited her a few days later.

It was a gray, cold, cloudy winter day in February, and the curtains were open in her room. I said hi, and her eyes opened. She asked me to close the curtains because the sunlight was so bright, it was making it hard to see me. This confused me somewhat. Then, out of the blue, she started talking, and I realized it wasn't to me. She was having a conversation with my grandpa, her husband. Tears ran down her face. She said how much she missed him and reached her arms out. Once again, she asked me to help with the light that was shining so brightly in her room. I sat with her awhile, gave her a kiss, and told her I loved her. I realized I had been shown a very, very special gift from above. I went home. It was only hours later when Mom called and said Grandma was gone.

I thought of the times Mom had said and done bad things to her mother. At this moment, as Mom cried, I could feel the real daughter come through. She loved her mama. This passing would lead to another bad time for Mom. We thought that things would just go on with her sleeping most of the time. All of us kept working and carrying on with life, but mental illness does not stop; it just changes forms.

Mom didn't want to pick on Dad anymore, and for some reason, she wasn't finding it in herself to degrade me. She was completely caught up in her mother's death and trying to close the estate. I found her talking about the love she had for her brother and how her mom was so hard on him. It didn't make any sense to us kids, so we ignored what was being said. It became her obsession to talk about her brother's family now, and how others were verbally picking on him. She would carry on with stories and say how crooked his ex-wife's family was and how they would all steal things from him.

One day, in the mail, Mom received a legal paper from her attorney. Mom was dragged into a fight with her brother involving their mother's estate. Dad was furious with Mom's brother, because he should have realized all his sister had been through in life, struggling as she did with mental illness.

The family knew not to bring up subjects that were sensitive to Mom. The greed for money from Grandma's estate would push Mom and her brother into heated arguments. Lawyers were brought in, and Mom's mind started to unravel to new lows. The conversations from our mother made no sense at all. Again, people were out to destroy our family, and now they were even spying on her brother and making him do horrible things to her and the family.

Mom had come to a place in her mind where she could talk with me. We had a different kind of relationship now. She said things that were mixed up, and I just listened. I was going to care for her. I was her sounding board and friend.

I was clearly changing as well. I was looking at Mom as someone I had to take care of. I didn't believe she could make it without me. She just wanted someone to talk to about the thoughts running through her head. I knew Dad would love it if I helped. Mental illness, I could see, had exhausted him. He was getting quieter.

LIFE CAN CHANGE ON A DIME

O ne dreary day, a pickup pulled into my folks' yard. A gentleman got out and knocked on the door. He introduced himself and asked if he could use the phone. "Come on in," Dad said. Dad looked past the man and saw a shadow in the pickup. He assumed someone was in there waiting. "Your wife can come in and wait in the house, too."

The man laughed as he said, "That's okay. It's just my dog." They all laughed. He told my folks he wasn't married and was a dentist in a nearby town.

I was working at a nursing home as a nurse's aide at that time. I picked up the kids from my sister-in-law's place and came home like any normal day. Dad came over, as usual, to see us. We were having small talk when he said, "I think we should take the kids for a dental checkup." I looked at him with wonder. Where did that come from? Knowing the money was tight for me, he offered to pay for the visit. I thanked him, not knowing he was trying to play matchmaker.

The following week, it was time for their dental appointment. The receptionist took the kids back to the exam rooms, as

Dad and I sat in the lobby. Waiting there, reading a magazine, I was totally enjoying the quiet moment. Dad said, "Get back there with the kids. They are probably scared."

"What? You're kidding, right? They're just fine. It's better if I'm not standing over them."

Dad was adamant. "Get back there."

"Good God!" I said. "All right." I walked down the hallway, and they had my daughter and son across from each other in different rooms. I stood in the hall and let them both know I was right there. I could see the lobby and my father sitting in the chair looking right at me. I looked at him and shrugged. He waved his hand at me as if to say, "Stay. Don't leave them."

As I stood there, I thought, *Wow, kids, Grandpa is getting overprotective.* A door opened, and the dentist came in to examine the kids.

He introduced himself. "That must be your dad?" I was stunned. How in the world did he know my dad? They proceeded to finish with the exams, and the hygienist cleaned their teeth. Then the dentist came out into the hallway, where I stood, and told me how well behaved and nice they were. He asked what I did and said it was very nice to meet me. I thanked him. I saw him go into the lobby to talk with my dad. I couldn't wait to get this figured out! We thanked the ladies in the office, got free toothbrushes, and left.

As we were driving home, Dad started asking me questions. "What did he say to you?"

"Not much. I have great kids. Why?"

"Well, I was just wondering."

I asked how he knew the dentist.

"Oh, his pickup quit working on the highway, and he stopped in our yard to use the phone."

I never said anything more. We just went home. I worked the next day. That evening, Dad called and asked me if the dentist had called me yet.

"Who?"

"The dentist."

"Oh my word, Dad. Really?" I asked him why he would ask me that.

"Well, he's not married."

Suddenly, things made perfect sense to me. For the next couple of days, I got the same phone call from Dad. He asked the same question, and I gave him the same answer. It was a Friday night. It was past 7:30 and Dad hadn't called. I was somewhat relieved. The thought of the dentist calling started to make me hopeful for some reason.

It was getting late, and the phone rang. I thought it was my dad. I picked up, ready to laugh and put his mind to rest for the evening. To my shock, it was a different man's voice.

"Hi. This is your kids' dentist." He made small talk. I found myself not able to speak much. My head was spinning. "I was wondering if you would join me for dinner tomorrow evening?"

I said I would like that, and we hung up. I waited a bit, knowing I had to call my dad. The phone rang. When he picked up, he sounded tired. I started to have small talk with him, but he was getting short with me and wanted to go to bed.

That's when I let him have it. "Would you be able to watch the kids tomorrow evening for a couple of hours?" That was met with dead silence, so I continued, "Your plan worked for at least one date."

I heard him yell to Mom, "He phoned her, and they have a date! We have to watch the kids." Then he hung up.

Looking at the phone, I thought, *Wow, I think he's more excited than I am.*

I was nervous about my first date. I was a closet smoker, so I had to make sure I didn't have smoke breath. It was hard not to sneak one before the date. I watched through the window as he pulled up. He was a gentleman. He opened my door to the pickup, and off we went to the Legion Club. It was known for its wonderful food and music on Saturday nights.

I was very happy, and we were getting along just fine. I felt pretty and confident. I had on a new outfit, and I knew I had gotten my body back into shape after having children. I was in a good place and out on a wonderful date. We danced, finished our meal, and were enjoying the end of the evening when out of nowhere he said, "You know you are a very beautiful woman." I thanked him, and with a pause, he said, "You would be even prettier if you lost fifteen pounds or so. I can help you with that."

I was silent and mortified. I couldn't say anything. I couldn't talk. I was frozen. "I hope I haven't hurt your feelings," he said. "I just wanted you to know I see potential." I looked down at my soft, pretty gray-and-white sweater and my cream-colored pants, thinking how pretty I thought it was on me.

My whole life was running through my mind in seconds. I wanted to cry and run away. I was retreating fast. Inside, I could hear my mind telling me, *Say something. Do anything so he will like you and be your friend. You know you're worthless, and you don't want him to leave. You don't want to disappoint Dad!*

As my mind was spinning, I heard, "Are you okay?"

I looked at him and said, "You're right. How did you know I have been trying to lose the last fifteen pounds from having kids and it's been tough?"

He looked at me with a gleam of happiness, and was excited that he was going to help me reshape my body.

I couldn't wait to get home and smoke! Thoughts were running through my head. *I'd better hang on to him. He's a great catch. I have kids, and I'm alone. I'd better get the weight off!* My regimen began.

He suggested I start running before work. I had to be at work by 5:30 a.m., so I was jogging in the dark. I wondered if Dad would like knowing I was running past his house at 4:00 in the morning to get the dentist's weight off.

He had me on a diet of cleansing drinks and no food for a couple of weeks. He said it would clean my digestive system out. I know this wasn't bad for me, and getting into great shape was good; however, I questioned his motives. Managing my body became his second job.

Once again, I fell into the trap of wanting to please. Kind words bolstered my low self-esteem. My weakness of wanting to be loved returned. I got super-skinny to make him happy.

My kids really liked him, and I let myself believe that this must be what love was. We had fun. I accepted my new requirement to keep in shape. I didn't want anything to ruin our new life. I didn't think then that I was returning to old patterns, replacing my mother with this man.

At the same time, Mom was still drinking beer and having trouble dealing with the money and estate issues.

Dad was excited for me to be dating this gentleman. He had a child of his own and was a very successful man. He loved horses and roping, and the family was welcoming. I kept his secret of getting me skinny. Another scar on my soul that I would have to endure.

The children and I loved living on the family farm, our homes were walking distance from each other. Mom enjoyed coming over to my place to play with her grandkids on days I had off. She tired easily, and frequently, she would lie down on our sofa and take a nap while the kids were napping. Sometimes, I watched my mom lying there and wondered who she really was and how it might have been if she weren't ill. I kept thinking in the back of my mind that all the pills and beer she was consuming could not be good. Why had no one found a cure for this horrible illness?

Months went by. I was surprised when the dentist asked me to marry him. I applied for a job at the veterinary clinic in the town we would be moving to. I was so grateful to get the job. He wanted to adopt my children. We were going to be a new, happy family. I was too distracted to think much about Mom, and that was a relief. I knew things would stay the same with her, so I put a Band-Aid on her in my mind. I just wanted to enjoy this happy moment in my life.

The wedding day arrived. I chose to walk down the aisle with my two little children, and we walked together toward our new future. My heart was full of joy. I really believed this was going to be the wonderful ending to the long life of mental abuse I had been living.

When the service was over, I looked at my mom, and she was sobbing. I wondered what was going through her mind. I asked Dad later that evening, and he responded, "Mom said she had never seen you that happy, but at the same time, she didn't want you to leave her and move." It was breaking her heart.

We had a very intimate wedding—just immediate family. This was followed by a very large reception at the Ord Veterans

Club, and it was packed. We hired my boss's band. People packed in. Small towns love a free wedding dance. We were enjoying our family and friends in our new town, close to his dental practice.

When it came time to have wedding cake, I looked into his eyes as he put a bite of cake in my mouth. I wondered if seeing me eat all those calories bugged him. To please him, instead of going and sitting with friends and eating our cake, I suggested we sit at an empty table. I pushed my plate toward him and said, "Throw this away so no one sees." I didn't eat it. He smiled and did just that. Everyone, including the kids, were dancing and having a wonderful time.

We honeymooned in Breckenridge, Colorado. I hugged the kids. It was hurting me to leave them because they were so young, but I knew my family would take good care of them.

Things seemed so right at this moment. I was so thrilled for the children, and I wanted their normal to be so different from mine. I looked forward to making all of us a happy family.

On the first night of our honeymoon, we decided to spend the night halfway, rather than driving the whole way. I don't recall the name of the town, but the memory of that night still haunts me.

We had been sleeping together for the past six months, so nothing would be new, but knowing he was my husband gave me a different feeling of comfort. It was a secure sense of belonging I hadn't ever felt before. I loved this man, but I still possessed an emptiness I couldn't explain.

The night was special, and a sense of peace came over me. We got up and readied to finish our drive the next morning. At breakfast, he had the same look on his face as he did on our first date. I asked him if something was wrong. My heart was beating hard. I knew pain was going to enter it again. He started by saying, "I am so glad you lost all that weight. You look incredible!"

I put my hand on his arm and thanked him for his help. I told him I felt beautiful. I praised him for being right, a little weight loss can change someone's happiness and appearance. I took a sip of coffee, and then he said, "But you know what has happened by you being so heavy when you were pregnant? You carried extra weight. And now you're so skinny, your boobs are really ugly to me. They're flat like pancakes. I have trouble wanting you sexually because they are so ugly." I couldn't move. I sat looking at the saltshaker. He continued, "I think we should get you breast implants. You know, to fill in the emptiness."

I wanted to hide my chest. I couldn't believe this man, my husband for less than twenty-four hours, was saying how ugly my breasts were to him. I was terrified he would leave me, but at the same time, I hated him for those words.

"Are you okay getting your boobs done?"

"Why are you saying this to me now?" I asked, stunned.

"Well, I have it already arranged. We go skiing for a day, do a little sightseeing, and then go to Denver. I have an appointment with a plastic surgeon already lined up. We can get it all done before we go home."

I felt like I had been beaten with a long stick. My smile vanished from my face. I couldn't even say the word *no*.

"Are you all right with this?"

I looked at him, and the words came out with no effort at all. "Sure, whatever you want, if that will make you happy." He got up from the table like he had won the Powerball and went to make the phone call to confirm my appointment.

We went to Breckenridge. I found myself putting on a T-shirt for bed. I was ashamed of my breasts now. Deep down, I thought, *I lost the weight for him, and now I have to fix my flat chest. What's next?*

I didn't want to be naked. I wasn't feeling the same love I had felt the day before. We went down to get into the hot tub. He was trying to play footsie with me. I never said a word, but I moved my foot away from his. Now, not only was I constantly hungry and afraid to put food in my mouth, I also had to feel like my body was ugly.

We skied all the next day, and he was at the height of glory, smiling, and having a great time. I knew the drill: put a smile on my face, act like I was over the moon with joy, and lock the sadness up in my heart.

The familiar feelings came back to me as I took in the rugged, breathtaking Rocky Mountains.

I didn't feel good about myself. I was nothing again, not good enough for anyone, just a simple, stupid girl. For some reason, I felt warm around these mountains, like they were calling me home. I had no idea why, but I was at peace there, standing atop a mountain, by myself, as if there was more to this world.

The next day, we drove into the city of Denver, Colorado. I looked at every tall building and felt, momentarily, captivated by its beauty. Then, I remembered why we were there, and I started to feel scared and empty inside. We parked, and I walked toward my fate. The damp air seemed to have a raw chill to it.

The doctor came into the room. I had to take off my bra. I said nothing at all. I was listening to my husband and the doctor discuss the size I should be to get rid of the loose, floppy look. When this strange man touched my breasts to examine them,

I left my body, as I had when I was little and my mom would beat me with a stick. I made my body not feel. I couldn't feel the moving of my skin while they were lifting my breast like it was just a slab of meat. I watched as the two of them shook hands, never asking me for my input. I dressed as they talked about the time of the surgery the next day and how I wasn't supposed to eat anything the night before. I know that the doctor didn't understand when I turned and said, "Not eat? That won't be a problem." I was cold inside. I wasn't sure what was going on in my mind or heart at that moment.

It was the day of the surgery. I was almost glad I was going to be put under. I hadn't really slept well since I was told how ugly my breasts were. During the night, I found myself touching each breast and feeling the warmth from my skin. I felt scared for my body.

Before surgery, my husband told me he had gotten a call from his ex-wife, who said he could have his daughter for a couple of weeks. He would have to come get her. They lived in Phoenix. I was going to learn how much his daughter ranked over me . . . and everything else. He said, "Well, you're going to be in surgery and sleeping most of today, so I booked a round-trip flight to Phoenix. I will return tonight with my daughter."

I didn't say a word. I was shell-shocked from everything. *What's one more thing? You don't want to be with me when I have your surgery? Fine. Why not.* I was very quiet. He waited until they took me back, and he was gone.

The nurse came in and was very nice. She asked me where I was from as she put the needle in my vein. I looked at her and said, "I am on my honeymoon, and he wants my boobs pretty." As I was starting to shut my eyes, I could feel her warm hand squeeze my arm and then gently touch my face. My eyes closed, but I could still hear another woman come into the room. I heard what she said: "I can't believe he left her and it's their honeymoon."

The next thing I knew, I was trying to open my eyes, but it wasn't working. I heard a loud alarm and people scrambling and talking. I wanted to say something. My body was being moved around, and there was pressure on my chest. I could hear the nurse calling my name and saying, "Breathe! Take deep breaths! Come on, Karen, you got this. Wake up! Fight!"

Because of the sedation from the anesthetic, I wasn't breathing in enough oxygen. My blood pressure fell, and my entire body was dangerously slowing down. I could only hear the machine screaming in my ear. I must have lost consciousness for a while. Then I could hear the nurse calling my name again, and this time, I got my eyes open. There was my nurse. She was still there for me. I was relieved and asked her how it went. She held my hand. "He should be pleased." Then, she rolled her eyes as if to say, "I have you, sister." As she stood watching the machine displaying all of my vitals, she said, "You know, sister, you almost bit it just for his boobs." I felt so close to her. We could have become friends if I lived there. I noticed she wouldn't leave me. It was an unspeakable bond. She was my angel through this.

I could finally sit up, and she said, "I hope he gets here soon. This is an outpatient hospital. You have to be checked out in an hour."

I looked at her. "I can get myself to the hotel if I have to."

She looked back at me and said, "I bet you could!" with a big smile. The door opened, and there was the receptionist.

"There is a gentleman in the lobby with a little girl. Do they belong to you?"

I looked at her and looked at my nurse and said, "I suppose they do."

"Well, he can't come back here with her, so we are supposed to get you ready. I will walk you out."

I was pissed off, but I believed I couldn't share my feelings with anyone, and I should be grateful for this life with him.

I walked out into the lobby, and my chest felt heavy. I saw his three-year-old daughter, gave her a little hug, and off to the hotel we went. I had a follow-up appointment in the morning. I would be released, and we would go back to Nebraska as though nothing had happened.

That night, my chest felt like it was burning. I couldn't tell if it was surgery or my anger making me hurt so bad. I never once complained; I took my pain. I was trying to grasp what had actually happened over the past three days.

He slept in the other bed with his daughter, and I was alone once again. I had many depressing thoughts and one familiar one. It was the feeling I'd had all my life of being unwanted and degraded. When we got home, the story was supposed to be that I had a skiing accident and was swollen from the injury. That's what I agreed to tell everyone so no one would know what really occurred.

It was wonderful to hold my kids again. We started living in my double-wide trailer. It was larger than his house, but I knew we would be moving because of the horses and his dental practice. I couldn't help but think of my mother, and it started to hurt deep inside me that the kids and I were leaving. It wasn't far, just sixteen miles. But what was only a short distance for some was too far for my mom. She and I had become close in such a different way. I was now her friend.

CHANGE FOR MOM

After all Mom's mental breakdowns, no one, apart from a woman named Emily, would come to visit her. Old friends, neighbors, and church ladies had all abandoned her. Emily was the wife of the man Dad had once rented farmland from. She understood that Mom was mentally ill. She visited with Mom as if there wasn't anything wrong at all. Mom so looked forward to her visits.

Mom was never invited to any town functions anymore. I had to wrap my mind around the fact that people treat someone with mental illness differently from someone with physical illness. Cancer and other diseases don't disqualify a person from inclusion the way mental illness can.

My memories of our special days, one in particular, came rushing back to me. We didn't experience many, which is why I could remember each one so vividly.

One day, I took Mom about a hundred miles away to a bigger town where we could go shopping. She bought things she needed, and things she didn't need, and loved it. She went down each aisle as if she had never seen such merchandise. I pushed the cart behind her, watching her talk to herself. "Oh, I really like this shower curtain. It's such a pretty color." This went on and on until she said she was done. We had the best afternoon. Even with her illness, some pleasure came to her on this day.

Mom and I talked on the phone every day. I had to work at my husband's office, but I always took time to visit with her. Life seemed simple now. Mom would still say strange things sometimes, and Dad said she slept every afternoon like clockwork. I was raising my kids and had a good, simple marriage going at this time. All seemed calm.

It's a common fact that people learn, as I did, to hide their feelings and thoughts way down deep. So deep, they can think they're fine and that all the scars have gone. I did this and managed, sometimes, to fool myself.

Mom was again saying things that didn't make sense. She talked about her brother, and the estate issues, and his divorced wife. Some of it was sensible, but it was getting to be repetitive. Our phone calls became ones where Mom would say, "You're the only one that will listen to me." I always let her talk, even if it was off the wall, like the moments when she still insisted flowers had to be yellow and people were making fun of her blue car. Then she'd reprise the stories of people hurting my dad without him knowing it. This was a change from constantly calling him dumb and yelling at him for not believing what she said. It used to be pure hate from her mouth, but now it was pure sympathy for Dad.

One afternoon, Dad called and told me to get right home because something was wrong with Mom. I drove to the house as fast as I could and found Mom sitting in the kitchen chair glaring. She wouldn't talk. Her eyes were full of water, very milky looking. I told Dad I thought she had a stroke and we needed to get her to the hospital. I tried to talk to her, and she just looked at us without changing her facial expression. We took her down to the local hospital. She wasn't saying much, just staring off into space. The doctor thought she may have had a stroke as well, so she was admitted to the hospital.

When I was visiting her one afternoon, she asked me if I would shave her legs. I got a pan from the nurse and started to shave Mom's legs. As I was doing this, she said, "I love you," as she touched my head. My heart melted at this moment. I had waited my whole life for Mom to talk to me this way. The look in her eyes was beautiful, warm, and loving. It is incredible that after living twenty-eight years of thinking my mom didn't love me, rationalizing her illness, and giving her the free pass of being sick, those words could still mean so much to me. I realized how painfully I had been waiting for this moment.

Every part of my body relaxed. I took my time shaving her legs. I could tell it had been forever since she'd shaved, but I didn't mind at all. I was like the Grinch; my heart began to grow, screaming out, "I love you, too, Mom." There will never be words to explain that moment, but the healing was beginning. It was like an out-of-body experience. I gave Mom a hug. I almost couldn't leave her there that day; I wanted to take her home with me. I had so much I wanted to talk about and tell her. The hate eased up inside of me. I thought Mom was 100 percent cured. My mom was real, and she had come back to me. I went into a fantasy that all was great and wonderful. I was overcome with joy. My mind refused to deal with reality that day.

Reality would soon return. Mom's illness would take over. Dad got her home, but there was never a diagnosis for her catatonic state. A small, local hospital cannot train for the entire world of mental illness and all the signs that come with it. Mom just got sent home. More drugs were always prescribed.

Mom continued to call me almost every day. Sometimes I wouldn't answer. I had become her sounding board, the person who would listen to her and not tell her she was crazy or wasn't making sense. There were days I just didn't have the strength to go through this charade. It's difficult to carry a conversation that consists of the way a car was parked or why some people had been walking the wrong way on the sidewalk. Her primary focus was her brother and the land payment, and wondering why he wouldn't just end the estate battle.

Sometimes she would go to the local café for lunch. She would notice how only certain plates were used for eating, and she thought this was a sign of some conspiracy. She had to sit at a certain table, facing a direction that was "safe" in her mind. She would visit with the waitress and start talking about Dad. It wasn't how stupid he was; it was sympathy for him, because people were hurting him and he didn't know it. Mom would say, "I need to help Richard because they are going to change him." I wondered how the waitresses handled Mom on her visits.

Darkness was coming, but we couldn't see it yet. Ticking time bombs in mental illness are not visible to anyone. It is difficult when you cannot and do not know what the person is thinking.

I took Mom to her doctor appointments back in Hastings, where they had dealt with her mental illness before. The answer was *always* medication. I came to believe that in their minds, it was best to turn the person into a zombie, virtually trance-like. Mom took her medications, and she could function, doing housework and making meals, but she was like a robot. She had become silent, thinking only to herself.

Dad said Mom was sleeping more often during the day, taking naps in the morning, and sleeping all afternoon. We didn't know Mom was on a medication overload. She was on so many drugs they were contradicting each other. There was a complete warfare inside of her. Time went by. Dad worked, Mom napped. About once a week, she would call, and I would let her talk. I noticed phone calls weren't every day like they used to be.

Sometimes, we went up to help my father move cows from different pastures. Mom always had a very nice meal waiting for us when we finished. Other times, we would go visit just to say hi. Once, I noticed Mom staring at me and my hair. I could feel her returning to the place where she would say hurtful things to me. The difference now was that I could see it, but Mom didn't say anything out loud.

Even so, our family did enjoy celebrating Christmas. The most special one was when Dad and Mom came over, and we surprised her with her first microwave. She was so intrigued with it.

Mom loved to play pitch with all of us. If there was someone who played incorrectly, she would either laugh until she cried, or, if it was her team that made the mistake, she would let that person have it verbally: "Why did you play that?"

Through all of this, my brother, sister, and I never talked among ourselves about Mom. At this point, I had no idea what they were thinking about the journey Mom had been on with this illness.

In January 1986, Mom said, "I feel something is coming. I don't want to get sick again." Mom could now tell when things were going wrong in her body. When she was clear in her mind, she would read huge medical books about mental illness and treatments. Often, on her table, there would be an article she had circled and highlighted with a yellow marker.

She had a journal from Dorothea Dix, a social reformer who became an advocate for the indigent insane and was instrumental in creating the first American mental asylum. Another one of Mom's journals, written by Wulf Rössler, was titled *Stigma of Mental Health*. Rössler said, "Overall, the 1960s and 1970s were full of an anti-psychiatry attitude, blaming psychiatry for being repressive, coercive, and more damaging than helpful to patients." This portrays the idea that mental health wasn't important and shouldn't even be discussed. Rössler talks about the way mental health is portrayed negatively in the media, for example, in the movie *One Flew Over the Cuckoo's Nest*. In the 1960s, many critics of psychiatry emerged, such as psychiatrist Thomas Szasz, who argues that schizophrenia doesn't exist. Erving Goffman claimed most people in mental hospitals exhibited psychotic symptoms as a result of their hospitalizations. Ken Kesey said, "Patients don't have mental illness, but rather, they simply act in ways society deems unacceptable."

It was time for a checkup with the doctor. They assigned Mom a new doctor, and I drove her to the appointment. I didn't know that it would be her last-ever doctor visit. We went to the new doctor's office. The doctor spent just fifteen minutes with my mom. I asked if Mom's fifteen pills were too many and whether they could be interacting negatively. The doctor decided to take Mom off all her medications at once and told her to return in one month. He would check on her then and begin a new medication protocol. We left more confused than when we'd arrived.

I thought it was unwise of him to make that decision after just one fifteen-minute office call. It felt as if this facility ran mental patients in like cattle, talked about pills, and then sent them on their way. This seemed to be standard practice during Mom's battle with this horrible illness.

If I had only known that a mentally ill person should never have all their drugs removed at once. Later, I spoke with my doctor, who explained it as "a medicine warfare" going on inside the body.

Some pills were supposed to calm her; others were supposed to promote activity in the brain. It was like ten different signals were being sent to my mother's brain every day. The body can go into a chemical shock if all drugs are removed at once. A person can spiral in so many different directions.

Mom was fine for a couple of days; she actually did really well. Then we noticed that while her conversation was fine, her manner was nervous. She completely stopped napping and was always doing something in the house. She couldn't sit still. Dad was concerned and felt she needed something like a calming drug.

One evening, Mom drove down to our house. She never liked driving at night, but there she was. Mom ran drug names by my husband and asked him what they did. She was still determined to figure it out. She wanted to know what was going on and what she had been directed or prescribed to take. I wish I had then the knowledge I have today. That was the last time my family would see her alive.

AFTER THE FUNERAL

A t my mother's grave site, my father cried. "I hope that
the demon in Mom's mind who took her away from
us dies with her and never raises its ugly head to any
of our family."

My sister and I went once each week to clean his house and
to cook some food for the week ahead. It was incredibly difficult
for months. Dad didn't let us do anything with Mom's clothes.
He said he wanted to smell her every day, and if the clothes were
there, it felt as if she were, too. Watching true love hurt that way
was sometimes more than I could take.

My son, who was only seven, sometimes came with me.

"Mom, Grandpa is crying in his bedroom." I told him how
much he missed Grandma. Sometimes, when my kids came with
me, they would hold my dad's hand and say nothing. He would play
card games with them. I knew he hurt so badly behind that smile.

Our first Christmas without her came eleven months after
her death. It was truly raw for us. We all pitched in to give Dad
a new leather recliner. He loved it, sat in it, and then all of a
sudden, he got up and left the room. It took a moment to realize

that he was in the bedroom crying. It would take a long time for all of us to be able to smile again.

Meanwhile, I was hurting, carrying so much guilt about my mother. I still thought of the days she looked at me with disgust and how far we had come before she died. My husband and I started to drift apart. There was no reason. I didn't understand, but I had no strength to ask why or wonder what was going on. We would only really connect if sexual urges arose. I quit looking for romance in our marriage. I kept in line by being thin and slim. I would carry on with daily chores and taking care of meals and housework. My sister and I were getting closer, and that seemed to help fill my empty feeling inside.

The feelings from the life I lived as an abused child did not get buried with the abuser. I had no idea that Mom could leave this earth for heaven, and the nightmare of healing was still to come for me. I tried to discuss my thoughts and feelings with my husband. To my surprise, he didn't want to talk to me about it. He said, "Bury it with your mom. Be done with it."

When I tried to talk with Dad, he didn't want anything to do with it either. He was done with that chapter of his life. Dad's way of dealing with it was by not talking about it. I know my father had his private moments, reflecting on the love of his life and the journey that they traveled. I am not sure of the weight he carried, but I know it was huge to stay as strong as he did. It was incredible to have watched and participated. There are no words to describe my father's commitment to that relationship; he had incredible integrity. We were all fortunate, and so was our mother.

I realized I had to look at my life. When I was dealing with my mom and all the things she was going through, I had no time to share with anyone what my life had become. The focus was always on Mom. Now that she was gone, I was lost inside. Life was about to show me what happens to a child who's been abused by the hands of mental illness. I still did not know who I was; it felt like something was living inside of me, like a demon. Mom and I had found love in our relationship, but for me, it came too late. I hated that Mom was gone. Our journey together had been improving. We could talk without it being so off-the-wall. I had started to enjoy her because the yelling and criticism had gone away.

Raising the kids, life was moving along. They were happy. Everything was well on the surface. I kept telling myself I could handle it for my children. I had to think of them. I would do this for years. I didn't say anything to anyone. I believed I wouldn't ever be right in my husband's eyes. I always did what he wanted and never questioned it. I thought, *I have a roof over my head and my babies are getting a good life, so be still.*

I was still in a routine of extreme exercise and eating very little. Something was slowly starting to rebel inside.

We had lived in my husband's small trailer for years by now. He asked me to come to one of the bedrooms where he had some items stored. As I walked in, he was holding up a pair of jeans. I could tell they were women's jeans. "Whose jeans are those?" I asked. He proceeded to explain to me that they were his ex-wife's jeans. He wanted me to see how tiny they were.

"When you can fit into these, you'll know you're thin enough. You will have reached your weight target." He handed them to me and said, "Keep them until they fit."

I could have died inside! My heart hurt. Carrying on with this life was going to be so hard.

For some reason, I let it get inside my head. I believed my spouse when he said that being thin was my way of being perfect. I slowed my eating down to hardly anything. I was starting to get severe headaches. The office had pain pills I could take. They became a part of my routine, along with working at the office and working out several times a day, trying to get into those special jeans.

I recalled one time before my mother's passing we had gone to my parents' house for dinner. My mother had made my favorite blueberry pie. She sliced everyone a piece and handed each one of us a plate.

In front of everyone, he pushed it away from me and said, "She doesn't need that." Everyone looked at him but said nothing.

My sister had come to visit me one afternoon and brought that time up to me. She proceeded to let me know she felt I was getting too thin. I could feel her concern. I reassured her I was taking care of myself.

I had already started taking Percocet, which is a narcotic, three times per day. It was easy to keep my bottle full working for a doctor. Eating one small meal a day (some fruit with yogurt) and working out three times per day in order to keep a Barbie-doll image consumed my every thought. I still couldn't stand up to him. I had no coping skills in my soul. We continued this for years, and my family noticed how thin I was. I always wondered what they said when I wasn't around.

I had a close friend from church ask me why I was getting so thin. What was I supposed to say? I needed to get the kids raised and then deal with me.

I watched my children have the time of their lives. They played sports, went to rodeos, swam, golfed, fished, and had vibrant groups of friends. I never ever had a problem putting myself on the back burner; I always loved watching them have fun no matter what.

By now, I didn't love my husband anymore. I had built a wall inside me. I was married, but living alone in my heart. I got involved with church, taught Sunday school, joined the Chamber, helped with events in the community, joined a ladies' golf league, and enjoyed going to school events. I managed to stay so busy that the days blew by just like the wind.

The mental abuse was still going strong. Now he didn't even have to deride me out loud; I had a silent hell in my mind. I think we both knew the marriage was ending, but I had to stay super thin no matter what. When I was trying to stay thin, I was drinking with my friends and smoking socially to help take the edge off. My friends would joke and say, "She never eats."

They had no idea I was living under my husband's watchful eye when it came to my weight.

I was building a mind-set of hate and resentment. The feelings I'd had when growing up with my mom were coming back. They were overtaking the good I'd had with her at the end. I was mentally putting my husband in the same box as my mom. "I will never be good enough for either of you, so why should I care?"

I had started a downward spiral of self-destruction, but I didn't know it yet. Alcohol and friends became my coping mechanism. For years, this game played out. My husband had his joys in life: calf roping, team roping. Practically every weekend, he would be gone. Our son loved this as well, and they would go together, creating a very special bond. Our daughter always had friends over. She had her sports and fun activities at school.

I hung with my friends. There wasn't much family time. All of us pretty much did what we wanted. I would go shopping for clothes, I never had enough clothes. Our daughter loved bringing a friend along, and we would spend a weekend shopping in the city.

Needless to say, our marriage was on a slow burn, disintegrating in front of us. I was getting fed up with being told what and how to be, so I started to stand up to my husband. I'd let him know when something didn't work for me anymore. I spent more time with my friends than with him.

His child from his previous marriage would come and spend summers with us. I would notice his child could do no wrong, but he had no problem disciplining mine, despite them being really good kids. I had no problem with discipline. The family dynamics were starting to unravel. Affairs started, and we had plenty of excuses for separate weekends. We were never together and lived in denial. When I started to rebel, it was with a vengeance. All that built-up hate was coming out. I truly didn't want things to go this way, but I couldn't live like that anymore. I was done with the games; I wanted to be free from it all. I was tired of living the character in his unreal story.

Finally, we separated, and I moved away. I wanted the kids to come, but with one in college and the other one wanting to finish the last year of high school with his friends, they stayed. He was their adoptive dad, so I moved by myself. The separation from my kids was almost unbearable. Leaving my husband wasn't; I didn't mind getting rid of the man who didn't love me.

The week I left, I was in a mental state of shock. I had no feelings about anything. I knew it destroyed my children; they didn't understand how I could leave.

I was very confused. I wanted to run away from everything again. I know now, but didn't know then, that I was, to some degree, mentally ill at this time. I likely had been for some time. I didn't have one rational thought of being a mom.

As I was leaving, my son ran to his bedroom crying. My daughter was sitting in her room. I had no one to turn to at this point, and I knew I had to go. It was hard on the children, seeing how happy their father was that I was leaving.

His girlfriend had already moved to our little town and was working at our practice. The marriage had really ended long before I left. I had already seen the change in the small town. People making judgments, picking sides as they always do. To protect our children, I kept quiet about our personal life.

In my heart, I knew I would be back again one day, stronger than ever. I wanted to scream out, "I am going away to get better for my children!" I drove away crying so hard I almost could not see the road. Everything I had endured with my mom and my life up to this point would make me keep driving. I had to endure for my children.

I didn't know I hadn't begun to heal yet. I only knew I was becoming abusive to myself. I was drinking too much and losing a grip on my life. I felt like I was bobbing in a rushing river with no lifeline. I didn't want anyone, including my children, to watch. As I drove, I thought about how confused they must be. I had so much I wanted to tell them.

I ran away to the end of Kansas, where I would find the most painful, yet awakening, beginning to the rest of my life.

WICHITA, KANSAS

I had some friends in Kansas whom I had met earlier in life. They had no way of knowing how mentally weak and confused I was. I have no idea to this day how I had the strength to move and to make the new people around me believe I was fine.

I removed all family, except for my children, from my thoughts. I carried their faces and lives with me daily. Maybe they're the reason I hung on. I constantly made trips back to Nebraska to see them and to make sure they were okay.

I am sure it was devastating to my kids, and it must have broken their hearts. I wanted to change their lives and mine, to make everything okay. The question was *how*?

I clearly had no idea what to do. My mind was so confused. I started off with my first mistake. The first thing I did was hook up with a father figure. He wanted to control me and know every move I made. I took it for some time, but I was building up such hate inside my head. I felt locked inside of a room I couldn't get out of. My mind was closing in on me. I was scared to even be with him. Almost every day, I would walk for miles just to escape the grip he had on me. I realized it was getting scary when he would call if I had been at my friends' too long or at the grocery store too long; my instincts were running high. Something kept telling me, *Get the hell out of here. Run.*

The fear of it all was overtaking my thoughts. I was desperately trying to pull myself together. I was experiencing signs of mental illness. My mind would go totally blank. I worried I was turning into a form of my mother. I started shutting off and shutting down. I just couldn't feel anything for anyone, including myself, anymore. In some ways, it was like I went somewhere in my mind and was creating a pretend world to live in. It seemed that I was acting out a character every day. I would get up and role-play that I didn't have a past or anyone in my life. I became a stranger to myself. I would look in the mirror and not even recognize the woman looking back. I am glad my family didn't see me at this time because they wouldn't have known what to do for me. I was just existing. I never quit praying for help.

I continued to struggle. I never thought I could hurt again the way I had while growing up. My family never phoned. I don't know to this day if they thought I had lost my mind or if they were mad I left. My dad and brother never reached out to me during this time. My sister would talk to me once in a while. When she called, I worked to convince her I was fine. I wondered at times if I belonged on this earth. Then my children would come racing into my mind and overtake the demon thoughts.

Eventually, my sister came to see me. It was terrible for her to see me that way. I had no money, no furniture to speak of, and no family around. To her, it was like I was a stray dog who had no idea what direction to go. She tried to take some control.

"We're getting some furniture today. A bed, a couch, a coffeepot, and a credit card."

I found myself quietly going along with this. I was engulfed with love for my sister. I felt I had no strength left inside of me at this moment. My sister had also brought me the washer and dryer that I got out of the divorce. She told me she believed I would find my way. When she left, I saw her cry. As she drove away, I wondered if she knew how lost I really was.

I am sure she felt she was saying good-bye to a sister she didn't know anymore. I didn't know the journey I was on, but I told her I couldn't go back. I had to find myself somehow. I would still make trips back to visit the kids, but I never stuck around to visit the rest of the family. The kids were my rope to life, and they didn't even know it.

One morning I awoke, and by the grace of God, I knew I had to find good people. I had to get away from the ones who were making me feel badly about myself. I thought of my friend and her career. I decided that day to start one thing: to get back to work and engage in life. First, I had to prove some things to myself. I knew I was smart, and I knew there wasn't anything I couldn't do if I put my mind to it. I decided I wanted to be a real estate broker like my friend. I purchased books and started studying. It took months, but I finally took the test and passed. I called my girlfriend to let her know I had accomplished my goal.

I knew no one in my family would understand why this meant the world to me. I wasn't dumb, and this gave me a glimpse of how I would have handled college. I could hear a voice telling me that I could accomplish anything I wanted. Real estate was the first of many lessons to come my way. It taught me how to get out in public, to deal with every kind of personality, and to become successful in business. It was a cutthroat business, but it was giving me self-satisfaction.

Was I mixed up? Of course I was. I just didn't know how badly. I always had so much fear; it was almost as if I was out of my body during this chapter of my life. I wanted desperately to succeed. The days went by fast; I drove to the real estate office and went to work. I would take any house listing no matter what the price. I was even selling and buying $20,000 homes.

I got one listing that brought me a lot of criticism and caused some inner anguish, but I kept that feeling deep inside. Every Friday, the Realtors in the office shared their new listings in case anyone else had a buyer. I announced I listed a home that also, back in the day, was one of the BTK (Bind, Torture, Kill) homes. A family had been murdered there. I heard giggles and whispers of "Good luck with that." My broker, the boss of the office, told me I might have made a mistake and wouldn't be able to sell it. He also warned that this may not have been good for my real estate career. I couldn't share with him that I needed money, and I didn't care if I had to sell a shack with no windows at this point. Soon, my coworkers found out how driven I was. I sold the BTK house, and went on to get several awards: Rookie of the Year, Million Dollar Award for Sales, Million Dollar Award for the Buyer side. I was becoming a successful Realtor.

I didn't have much money left after my bills were paid, so I stopped buying groceries. I found out that every Friday, the real estate office provided bagels, fruit, and cheese. I would load up, eat a great meal, and later in the morning, I would sneak the leftover food into my tote bag to take home. They had no idea I was using that as my food for the week.

My journey wasn't easy, but it had led me to a supportive work environment where I met a lot of positive people. I met fun ladies who became friends. They had no idea where I had come from or anything about my past, and I kept it that way. I walked the walk and dressed the part, so no one noticed it was always the same wardrobe. I couldn't buy anything new. Thank God, I stayed the same size so I could keep wearing the same clothes.

The nighttime was the worst. I would sit in my apartment, think of my kids, and pray they were okay and would someday understand. I don't know if they loved me at this time or were so confused about their mother that they didn't know what to think. I know I must have seemed like a crazy, selfish person.

I didn't know how to stop the war within me. I was driven to stay ahead of the demons in my mind. I don't know whether I was ill or not. I never went to a doctor because I didn't trust them. I saw how they had treated Mom, so who could blame me?

Somewhere inside me was the will to keep going. I still traveled back and forth from Kansas to Nebraska to see the children. When I saw them, there was a deeper kind of pain in my heart: an empty feeling, a lonely, hollow feeling. When I left to return to my new world, I cried for hours. I hated being away from them. I felt I was dying inside. In my mind, but never to their faces, I said, *Mama is trying to fix herself. Be patient, my children. I pray my road will lead me home to you someday.*

LARRY

ouses were coming my way. I was getting to be known in my field and was getting referred more and more often. Real estate was taking care of me and was also helping me to pay for my kids' schooling.

I started talking often with another Realtor at my office. He was a fun-loving guy. I didn't see him as a new man in my life. But as time went on, almost a year or so, we began to date. Deep down, I had no feelings of keeping him around forever. I was still trying to find myself and love myself for the first time.

Eventually, the kids were making trips to Kansas to see me, which were the most wonderful times in my life. Larry, my real estate friend, wanted to meet them. He had such a wonderful sense of humor and a way of saying things to the kids so they would understand what I was doing for a living. Larry was a very thoughtful man with a very big heart.

For example, the first time he came over to pick me up for a date, it was as if he knew I wasn't eating well. I couldn't tell anyone that in order to help the kids and take care of my bills, eating was at a bare minimum.

He walked into my apartment, looked around, and told me how nice it was. I could tell he was looking at my home closely. Then he went for my refrigerator. My heart almost stopped; he opened it and closed it, never saying a word. I found myself speechless. I am sure my face had to be every shade of red.

"Should we go?" he asked.

We left. I asked where he was taking me for supper and was so excited because I hadn't been to a restaurant in forever. I couldn't remember the last time I'd been out to eat. He said he was going to surprise me, but he had an errand to run first.

As we were driving, he pulled into the grocery store near my home. I thought he must need something. As he parked, he said, "Let's go." As we walked in, he grabbed the cart and said, "We are shopping tonight for your fridge before we do anything else. I suggest you pick out what you like to eat, or I will." I looked at him as tears began to build up, and all of a sudden, I was feeling compassion for this man. I didn't know what to say. He was always a quick wit and told me I could say, "Wow, you're a hell of a guy! I think I like you." He laughed so hard he made me laugh. After the groceries were put away, we went to a quiet place to eat. That's the first time a stranger had ever said, "I care about you. Tell me what is going on with you. I want to know about you."

Deep down, I still had my wall up, waiting for an insult to come out of his mouth.

I was going to let him get to know me slowly. I wasn't planning to start with the whole truth: my mom, my life, what had brought me here, why I'd run away. I planned to keep things simple and offer no details for a long time.

We became closer, but I still hadn't shared my past. He knew my mother had passed away, my father remarried, I divorced, and I had two wonderful, grown children. As far as I was concerned, that was enough.

I had never been able to trust anyone to know about my past. I still wasn't sure what was going on in my own head, let alone try to tell someone else about it. I had no experience showing my feelings on the outside. I could handle whatever someone wanted me to say or do to make them feel good. I just never let them in. That was the shield I created—my barrier, if you will—so people couldn't hurt me anymore. I wasn't going to allow it.

Larry and I continued dating, and I met his family. He was divorced as well and also had grown children. They didn't like their father moving on, and while I knew I wasn't going to hurt them in any way, I also knew it would take time for them to trust me. I understood their confusion, not wanting a new person in their father's life. I chose to be reserved and let them get to know me on their terms. It sounds easy, but it didn't work out that way.

I didn't know how to share with Larry how badly his children's rejection hurt me. It resurrected feelings from when I was little and felt unwanted. I couldn't find the words to tell him. I hated the feeling.

I remember thinking, *Is this my future? Am I supposed to marry this man?* He did make me laugh. I did love him. I just didn't know what to do with this twisted past inside of me.

Would I learn to live with it or bury it somehow? I prayed at night for answers.

One weekend, I went to my daughter's to help her move. It was at Christmastime, and I knew she needed alone time with her mom.

When I had returned to Wichita from helping my daughter, Larry was in a grumpy mood, which was somewhat puzzling to me. It wasn't the Larry I knew. I felt something was very wrong with the man I had fallen in love with. He wasn't behaving like the man I had come to cherish.

Finally, I asked what his problem was. He said he was jealous. He asked if I had someone else back in Nebraska. This floored me. I didn't even know what to say. "If you don't know me by now, and have to ask that, we have nothing."

It was so strange; it was as if he did a 180-degree turn. He replied, "I am sorry I said that. I have no idea where that came from; I just don't like being here without you."

The next thing I knew, he was down on his knee. He proposed to me. I didn't know this whirlwind was going to happen. He looked so happy. The grumpy man he'd been five minutes earlier was gone. At the time, I didn't know this could be a sign of a heart problem.

Larry always wore a smile and always made everyone around him smile. We had a blast together from the first day we met. My mind was able to be true and free with this man, and I knew he loved me very much. My life had made its turn to happiness. I would bury the past and get on with our future. He bonded with my children. He and my son both shared an interest in fast cars. He was honest and loving to my daughter. He always made her feel at ease and supported her goals. I did have deep feelings for him, and I loved him with all my heart, so I said yes.

We made trips back to Nebraska together so he could meet my family. My dad liked him immediately. Larry thought the world of my family, and he let them know it. At the same time, I was growing fond of his folks in Wichita. I thought how lucky I would be to have them in my family circle. Everything was falling into place as I'd prayed it would.

We decided that since we were both Realtors, we should rent a place for a few months and look at buying a house together.

I was nervous about moving in before we were married, only because I was still nervous about his children.

I had peace about my future. I enjoyed this time and started smiling again. I would let the world know I was happy. I finally gave myself permission to go on with life, to enjoy Larry, be happy, love the kids, and work hard. I wasn't thinking always of my past; I believed I could seal it up and never open Pandora's box again.

We found a place to rent for six months. It gave us time to look for a house. I moved in just after he did—five days, to be exact.

My best memory about that first week was that I got to cook supper, which I love to do. I made a great meal, and we sat down at our dining room table to eat. I couldn't remember the last time I'd sat down at my own table, with someone I loved, and enjoyed a meal. For perhaps the first time, I was able to breathe in a relaxed rhythm.

The first weekend was fun; my daughter came down, and we had VIP tickets for the premiere of *Titanic*. I loved this time, and I loved this moment. My family was coming together, and this meant the world to me. Larry knew how important the kids were to me and showed them how much he cared about them. I still felt a distance from his children, but time would have to help with that.

My life turned upside down one Tuesday morning. We woke up, and I went to the kitchen to start the coffee and make our favorite breakfast, a bagel with cream cheese and a slice of tomato. Larry ate his bagel and drank his coffee and juice. The news was on. I told Larry I needed to get to work, because I had to check in with some new clients.

All of a sudden, Larry put a pillow in front of his stomach and said he didn't feel well. I asked if I could get him anything. He thought he had heartburn. He asked me to get his bottle of

TUMS to see if that would help. Then, he looked at me with fear in his eyes. His eyes were clear and piercing, and he almost looked right through me. He said, "Can you please stay home with me? I really don't feel well."

I came toward him, sat down, held his hand, and said, "You bet." I started to say, "Maybe I should call a doctor or your mom." He grabbed my hand so tightly I thought it was going to break. He then let out a moan, a sound I will never forget as long as I live. I knew I had to get help. I jerked my hand away and yelled, "Larry, I am calling 9-1-1!"

I dialed and raced back to him, and at that moment, his eyes were bulging and his tongue was hanging out; he was gasping for air. He held on to my arms with a death grip. I told the dispatcher to get someone to our home quickly. She connected his mom on the phone, telling her to get over to our house, at the same time telling me to put him on the floor so I could start CPR. I don't know how I lifted him, but I got him on the floor and started breathing into his mouth. I pumped his chest. I could see the color of his face changing to purple. I was frantic, trying desperately to help him. I kept breathing into his mouth and pushing down on his chest, going back and forth as the dispatcher directed me.

I looked up and saw the door opening. "Larry, hang on, they're here to help you!" The paramedics came racing through the door. I moved so they could work. His mom and dad came running in and started screaming, "Larry, stay with us!" His mom picked up the phone, which was still lying by Larry's side, and called his grandpa, who was a minister. All she could manage to say with a cracking, crying sound was, "Pray, Dad." She kept repeating that. I stood there watching while they hooked him up to the medical equipment and loaded him into the ambulance. I don't remember how, but I found myself sitting in the front seat of the ambulance; I didn't even realize I was still in my sweats.

I kept asking them if he was going to be all right. No one said a word to me. I didn't know they couldn't. They didn't want me going crazy with the anguish of grief. The sirens were screaming loudly, and the ambulance was flying down the street going through stoplights like the wind! I was silently praying all would be okay, realizing how much I loved this man, and how he had brought me out of my darkness. He had saved me. *Was he leaving me alone? Was I going to be alone again?* We got to the hospital, and a nurse took me to a room away from Larry. She said they had to work on him, so I should stay right there. Someone would let me know how things were going.

Emptiness surrounded me. I sat there with no phone. No one was coming for me. I wondered where his mom and dad were.

Finally, I felt I had to find out what was going on. I needed to talk with someone. I needed to get some answers. I needed to call my dad.

I walked out of the room, and there was my boss from the real estate firm. "Are you okay?" he asked. Realization was about to hit me. He took me to the door by the ER surgical room where Larry was, and finally a doctor came out.

I looked at him as he said to my boss, "Jim, can you bring her down here to a room with the rest of the family? We have to talk."

In my heart, I thought maybe Larry would make it. Maybe he would need surgery, maybe he was in critical condition right now, but he would be okay. When we were going down the hall, the doctor looked at Jim and said, "You have to keep her here in the hallway by the room where the family is; she will be able to hear me. Some family members don't want her in the room."

Those words screamed in my mind and heart. I knew that wasn't how his mom and dad felt. I loved this man. He was my fiancé.

Every emotion I had felt of being unwanted my whole life raged inside me. I had done nothing wrong. All the memories came racing through my mind again. I was numbed by the words. "I am sorry. We did everything we could. Larry didn't make it. He has gone to be with God."

I don't remember how, but my boss got me into a wheelchair and took me back to the room. I lost control and started screaming down the hallway. "How could he be dead? Please, God! Don't take my Larry!"

Larry's grandma must have cared about me more than I knew. She had called a friend of Larry's and mine and said, "You'd better get to the hospital and help Karen; she is going to need you. Some family will not be good to her today." There was Patty. I was grateful to see her; I grabbed her tightly and held on.

I don't know how she did it, but because I wanted to see Larry and spend time with him, she got it done. I found myself in the ER room with Larry. I was stunned. I couldn't believe he was gone. I thought I could see him breathe. I felt him there, still. I told the nurse I thought there had been a mistake, because he was trying to breathe. I didn't know the body could move for a while after death. That's all it was. I held him, gave him a kiss, and couldn't think of anything but wanting to take him home. I kept my hand on his chest. I didn't want to leave. I thought of how his mom and dad had to be hurting so deeply. Larry had a younger sister who had died of cancer a few years earlier. My God, his mother had lost her only two children in just a couple of years.

Patty told me she would take me home. I asked, "What are they going to do with Larry?"

She let me know that the coroner would come to get him. "Where is his family?" She told me they had left the hospital. I said, "Well, I will not leave until Larry leaves. I will follow him to the car. He never left me alone, and I won't leave him alone. I will stand by him as long as I can."

I sat and waited what seemed like hours. I know it wasn't. Patty squeezed my hand and said, "Here we go, I will walk with you." They came by me with the cart; Larry was in a body bag. I asked the coroner for permission to walk with Larry. I walked behind the cart and wished my Larry weren't in the black bag and that there had been some mistake. As the gentleman was loading him into the back of the car, I couldn't tell if I was even standing. I couldn't feel anything at all.

Once again, I was alone. The emptiness overwhelmed me. Patty kindly got me back to my home. As she drove, I couldn't speak at all; words wouldn't come.

When we walked in, I realized just how kind my coworkers were. They had come in and cleaned my living room so I wouldn't be reminded of what had happened just hours earlier. Larry had thrown up, but all evidence of that was gone. I looked at our office receptionist, who had come in and done this for me, and hugged her tightly. I couldn't talk with anyone. I couldn't deal with the agony, the lonely, empty feeling, the pain of all my life returning. My friends wanted to help, but I just needed to be alone for a moment. I asked them to come back in a while; I needed time to absorb it all. They respected my wishes and said they would come back later in the afternoon.

When I heard the door shut, all I could do was hit the floor and scream in despair. I cried from the depths of my soul. I got on the phone to call my dad and yelled out, "Larry is gone,

Dad! He died!"

Dad said, "Shirley and I will go get the kids and come to you."

I needed a shower. I had to get cleaned up; I wanted to wash the day away. I had to hang on to doorknobs to get from room to room. I cried out as the water fell on me. I couldn't feel my skin; I couldn't feel the water hitting my body. Somehow I managed to get dressed, and then all I could do was sit and stare with a hollow emptiness inside of me.

My father, stepmom, and children were there for me. My sister also came down. All of them stayed with me through the funeral. I had never experienced such public pain as that funeral. With Mom, it happened in the house, behind closed doors. No one really knew what our "normal" was. When we were in public, we pretended all was fine. I was trying to find a way to work through my grief, begin the healing process, and, somewhere in it, find *me* again.

I had such low self-esteem from living with a parent with mental illness. When a sense of worthlessness is established so strongly in childhood, it can stay with a person her whole life, unless she is lucky enough to have received help while still very young. Because I didn't believe in myself, life's obstacles were almost too difficult to cope with. I didn't know how to hang on and move through them.

The funeral was emotionally devastating for me. I would have been Larry's wife in just a few short months. We had locked in the church, minister, reception, paid the down payment on the food and rooms. The rings had been purchased. I was in such grief, I wasn't aware of the things happening around me. In the obituary part of the newspaper, my name was left off the list of his survivors. Later, I learned his parents made the children redo it, and I was named in the next day's paper. I wasn't yet aware of just how much his folks cared about me.

My family and I were placed in the back of the church for the service. I couldn't even see the casket. Then, to top it off, at the graveside service, I wasn't allowed to sit on a chair by the casket. I had to stand in the back of the tent as if I were not a part of this man's life. I had brought him happiness, laughter, and love again. Somehow the decision was made to separate me from the man I loved. The only connection I had to the service was that my son was asked to be a pallbearer. I am sure Larry's folks had something to do with that decision.

All the people that Larry and I worked with, and all the friends we had made together, formed a line to come straight toward me in the back of the tent. One by one, they came and hugged me. Then I knew the happiness and love that Larry and I shared would not be forgotten.

I knew I still had my work alongside these wonderful people, and I had to get on with my life. Dad and Shirley took the kids home, and my sis had to leave as well. They all had to get back to their lives. I hated to see them go. I found it funny in a weird way that everyone just disappeared, and there I was. I couldn't run away from this.

To my astonishment, Larry's folks and all our friends decided to hold a second funeral for Larry. This one was intended to show respect for our relationship and the love we shared. I found this quite amusing because Larry did love the spotlight.

I was so moved by this, I had no words.

I managed to dress in a nice suit and drive myself to the church. It was a beautiful service, and it was at the church where his grandpa had ministered. They had a luncheon at our old hangout, and all our friends and coworkers attended. God bless all these people who had such warm and caring hearts. I was moved and will be forever thankful.

I found myself wondering if his mom and dad were going to leave me as well. I figured they would. Why would they stay now that Larry was gone? Alcohol came back into my life with a vengeance. I couldn't engage in life. I couldn't eat. I was numb.

A few days later, I received a phone call. It was Larry's mom, telling me they wanted to come visit. When they got there, I had no idea what they wanted to discuss. I was about to find out how much they truly cared about me.

I thought they would be like others in my life and leave, but they didn't. Over the following years, they played such an important role in my life. They helped me move out of the house where Larry passed and into a place I could afford by myself. They helped me understand I needed to get back to work. They invited me over to have supper with them or to go over on Sundays to kill some time. I appreciated that, because time wasn't my friend.

But in all truth, I wasn't well again. What they didn't know was that Larry's death was making me regress. I continued to hide from my feelings.

Sometimes, I would go to the grocery store and just push my cart slowly down each aisle so it would pass the time. I would do this for hours, look down, and the cart would be empty.

The only answered prayer beyond the help from Larry's parents came through my work. Larry and I had been sitting as Realtors on a subdivision, selling homes on empty lots. The owner of the subdivision said he liked how I worked. I think he felt sorry for me, and he liked Larry. He also knew I was good at selling homes. He was a tough old guy, but he said I could sit at the model home and sell the rest of the lots until they sold out. I saw a softer side to him, and I was very thankful. This arrangement kept me going for over a year. It was taking everything I had to meet people and convince them to buy. The memory of Larry wasn't leaving. I was working with the same people at the same office, seeing the same friends. It was like I was stuck. I decided to leave real estate and all my memories and friends. I went and got a job at a dental office. They were amazed by how little training I needed. It was a relief to see new people every day. I was starting to be aware this job was reminding me more and more of my past. I was feeling depressed, so I moved on.

A friend had told me I should work for this plastic surgeon, so I applied. His wife worked in the office as well. I knew the minute I met her I was in trouble. She had my mom's stare. She reminded me of my old boss at the pet shop. I was only there a short time. I knew I had to press on; this was not going to be my life.

Out of the blue, an old client I had sold a home to called and told me of a new job. "I have put in a good word for you." I was so nervous and grateful. I landed the job. It was a high-end billing director position for a cancer treatment center in Wichita. The company was based out of Tulsa, Oklahoma. The next thing I knew, I was learning all the coding requirements for cancer billing. I started to notice something about myself. I was responsible for two hospitals and one freestanding cancer treatment facility. I was making a great living. I had my own office suite downtown. I would still work real estate on the weekends just to stay busy. Time on my hands only let the darkness of my past in. *Workaholic* was an understatement. If I didn't have any homes to sell, I would work at a bowling alley selling pizzas on the weekend. I kept thinking of my children, and I knew I had to make it for them. I had to find my way.

COLORADO ON THE HORIZON

I t was a sunny Friday afternoon. Larry's mom called. "Please stop by when you're done with work. We will be on the back patio." I loved their covered back patio. It was so beautiful with the white lounge chairs looking over the gorgeous, big lawn. There they were, sitting with snacks and my favorite summer drink—a cold beer with two green olives. There was a pretty envelope lying on the table. "Pick it up and open it," she said. I looked inside and pulled out a birthday card, and something fell out. I reached for it and could see it was an airplane ticket. I looked at them both, puzzled. "We decided you need to go to Fort Collins and see your friends and have some fun."

I was speechless. I hugged them both, and the smile wouldn't leave my face. This was the best birthday present I'd ever received! I knew Larry's mom was my angel. I stayed that evening and had a wonderful meal. When I went to leave, I looked back at her and waved good night. I knew she couldn't hear me, but I said, "I love you." I was so overwhelmed at that moment, I had trouble focusing on my drive home as tears ran slowly down my face.

It was good to see my friends when they picked me up from the airport. They were surprised when they saw me. In trying to heal from Larry's passing, I found out what my body does with stress. I am sure my girlfriend about died! All the years she knew me, I was super thin. I hadn't told her my ex-husband liked his women on the skinny side. Anyway, they hugged me, I joked about being overweight, and that was the end of that discussion. I had a wonderful time with them. It was just like being home with familiar faces.

They knew only my past of living in Ord, my marriage, raising our kids, and that we had fun golfing. I'd never told them about my mother. My girlfriend was getting ready to give me a ride to the airport to return to Kansas when I told her I felt at home here. There was something spiritual about Colorado. It seemed to be calling to me for a reason.

Well, as fate would have it, my girlfriend said she had seen an ad in the paper that day for an office manager for a medical office, which would be right in my line of work. I ran the dental office the entire time I had been married. This would be perfect! We both laughed, and she said, "You should fill out the application and just see. What will it hurt?" So when I got back to Wichita, I did just that.

Except for Larry's parents, I was already pulling away from the people in Wichita. I wasn't happy, but I didn't know why. I came home from work on a Thursday, and there was a voice message from Fort Collins, "Please call us. We would like to set up an interview." I about threw up with excitement!

My life had a spark again. I was tired of being the person I was settling for, the old Karen: work, go to the bar, have a couple of drinks, hang out with old friends, go home, get up, and do it all over again.

A flame started burning within me to be strong and to press on with life. I told myself that I was not dead or dumb. I had made it this far. I had proven to myself that I was smart. I looked back at my accomplishments and saw some light at the end of the tunnel.

I called Larry's mom right away and told her about my interview. They said they'd drive me to Fort Collins themselves. They knew I couldn't afford to do it on my own with all the bills I had, and I was trying to help my daughter and son the best I could.

By now, my daughter had my first grandson and needed every extra penny I could give her. My son was going through college, and I was helping him out however I could. I knew I could make more money than I did here, so off we went. When we got there, Larry's mom surprised me and took me shopping, helping me find business attire for the interview. Since I had gained a lot of weight after Larry's death, I didn't have a lot of my own clothes to choose from.

What if I got the job? How could I afford the move? What if I didn't get the job and had to go back? So many thoughts went through my mind. I remembered Mom saying, "You can't do anything. You're so dumb. You're never going to amount to anything." Right then, I decided I had to win this interview. I had more to prove to my mother. Even though she was gone, I was still trying to show her what I was capable of achieving.

I met the gentleman who was doing the hiring. He was a nice young man. We hit it off right away. After the interview, I wanted Larry's folks to meet my old friends from Nebraska.

Even though we all had a great time, my pain returned. I didn't realize how being with people from the past would bring my past right back to me. My mind was flooded with negative thoughts. I'd endured years of Mom saying I would never amount to anything, and ex-husbands obsessing about my weight or telling me he couldn't stand my friends.

Later that evening, we all met for drinks, and I got buzzed. I drank to hide my nerves, to hide the little girl inside that was still so scared of life and didn't know how to deal with anything. I hid behind the drinks. I laughed a lot, hoping no one would ever know how I was feeling. My insecurities were raging inside of me.

Larry's mom had become more than a friend; it was like having a real mother around. When we got back to Wichita and were waiting to hear from Fort Collins, she sat me down and had a mother-daughter talk.

"You will not get far if you drink too much. Alcohol is not your friend."

She had a beautiful way of reaching inside me. I started to get lost in the beauty of this woman who loved and cared for me. Her face showed no sign of aging. Not one wrinkle. And her blue eyes had such warmth. I looked at her small hands as we talked. Her nails were always manicured, and her clothes accented her attractive figure. As I listened to her advice, I couldn't bring myself to tell her I was scared of life and wasn't sure of anything right now. The only thing I knew in that moment was that I loved her.

I hadn't shared what was going on with my dad yet. I loved Dad so much, but I wasn't sure where I stood in his world anymore. Was he now ashamed, because I left and moved away? Did he think I was crazy, too? I am sure he had his thoughts about me and the way I had left. I am sure he would recall the time I ran away from home.

I was headed to work when the phone rang. "Hi, this is Cindy. You have the job." I was thrilled! I was excited and scared at the same time. I was leaving behind my past in Wichita. This time, I didn't feel like I was running away. This time, I was running *to* something. I couldn't wait.

I called Larry's mom. Larry's folks were excited for me, but it was painful to think of leaving them. They were the only reason I wanted to stay, but I knew life was pulling me away. Larry's mom and I had gotten close, and my heart began to break. I had experienced what it could have been like with her as a mother. If my mom hadn't been sick, we would have gotten to do all the things moms and daughters do together. Larry's mom had given me a special gift of secure love and wisdom. Since Larry had passed, we both realized we needed each other. We went shopping or out to eat, and they often had me over for supper. She helped me write my résumé. She even did my children's résumés. The talks and laughter we had come to know and cherish would now be over a phone call and maybe an occasional visit. I loved that I finally felt emotion—even if it was my heart breaking.

I went to say good-bye to the people I had come to know. It was time for me to find where my life was supposed to go. Maybe I would finally find peace.

My friends were real estate brokers, and they had found me a nice place. I was moving to my new home sight unseen. I literally drove to my new home not having a clue where it was or what it looked like.

We pulled up, and it was just perfect. For the first time in my life, it felt as if things were working out. I had a job. I made the move. I had a new home. There wasn't a glitch in any of it. I had trouble trusting life, but I could trust this. It was like life lay down before me and said, "Follow this path."

Larry's folks were staying with me until I was settled. We got everything done. Larry's dad took me all over town so I could get my driver's license and a bank account. Larry's mom surprised me with new dishes and put my whole kitchen together. They even surprised me with a special gift: two Nebraska barstools. I was so moved by this I could hardly thank them enough. They made sure I had nothing to do except start my new job. Larry's mom took me shopping to get some great business wear. They were wonderful to me! There aren't enough words to describe these two wonderful human beings. There are angels in this world if you just open your eyes and look.

My kids knew I was moving, but they were busy with their college classes. I called my dad and stepmom; they seemed happy I was in Fort Collins. They loved that my old friends lived there, too. I think Dad was feeling relieved that I wasn't alone. I was forty years old and hoping this would be a great fit—that my life would finally become my own.

I found out later that Larry's mom had called my dad. She told him how much I needed this new start and that my soul needed to heal. As much as they hated to see me go, it was the right thing. Dad helped by sending money to move my things, and I told him in all my life, this was the best gift I'd ever received from him.

"Well, you never got to go to college like you wanted. The other two kids got to go, so it's only right I help you this way." Dad didn't forget those words I had spoken so long ago about wanting to go to college. He'd heard me. I was moved to the end of heaven and back. Still to this day, when I think of that moment with my dad, tears come, and warmth fills my heart.

It had come to the day when Larry's parents would leave and we would have to say good-bye to each other. I was ready for my new job, and it was time for them to go home. Larry's mom gave me a Bible with my name in it, which touched my soul. I loved having her in my life, and I really felt how much she loved me, too. We cried, and when they pulled away, I watched out the patio window. I saw her look back at me and wave with tears running down her face. We were meant to be together. God had brought us to each other. Both of her children were gone—including my Larry—and my mother was gone. We each had holes in our hearts that the other helped fill.

This feeling was touching the little girl inside me. My stomach didn't feel nervous when I was with her. I felt strong. She was my rock, and I knew she always would be.

They left on a Saturday, so I had a couple of days to hang out before starting work.

I paced the floor of my new condo. We had hung all my family pictures up. I started to look at my children's baby pictures and pictures from their graduation. Why couldn't I love myself? I thought every negative thing that went on in my children's life was my fault. I didn't know if it was the divorce that was making them feel lost or the fact I didn't live by them. All I knew was that in my heart, I was carrying guilt for them. Their sense of security was broken. I could hear it in their voices on the phone. They were distant. I knew somehow I had to make my life, and theirs, whole again.

I would stare out my window a lot and wonder what was going to happen to me. I was constantly saying over and over in my head, *Mind over matter.* I was fighting off the severe dark hole I would go to so often. The walls were caving in; I didn't like being alone. I didn't sleep well, waiting for my workweek to begin.

Monday came, and I started my new job. It was nerve-racking, like any other new job.

Everyone was really nice, but I could tell they didn't want to hang out together after work. For now, it was just going to be working relationships.

I was going over to my friends' house a lot, and I could feel that was starting to be an imposition. They had kids still at home, and their family life was quite different from the life of a single, divorced mother/grandmother. I knew not to put pressure on my friends. I needed to find my own way. I sometimes helped by watching the kids if they wanted to get away. I loved their family, and it was a secure feeling knowing they were there.

I made friends with the lady who lived above me, and we started walking five miles every night. I was also getting close to a few women at work. There was one woman at work I connected with instantly. We became almost inseparable. She was divorced at the time and had kids. We loved hanging out, doing everything together: walks, shopping, spending evenings together just to break up the time. I could tell we needed each other's friendship at that moment.

My evenings were somewhat difficult. I was sad I wasn't near my family. But in the same thought, I didn't know if they missed me at all. I drank in the evenings; I was trying to numb the pain that I still couldn't seem to shake.

My stomach returned to feeling like it had an electric mixer in it. I was settling into my own nervous little universe. I was starting slowly to understand that being alone wasn't so bad after all.

I was getting my home organized and letting my thoughts go where they wanted at nighttime. I was working on my inner self. I wanted to love myself and take pride in my accomplishments, but a demon of low self-esteem still lurked within me.

There was a really sweet girl at work, and she decided to play matchmaker one evening. I agreed to meet her friend. He seemed nice, polite, and had a sense of humor. My loneliness and desire for a friend caused me to see more in him then what was actually there.

I have no idea why I agreed to start dating him. Immediately, I saw things that bugged me. I was picking up on how much we didn't have in common and that there was something wrong with this person. I started to feel uneasy around him. I found myself wondering, *Was Mom right? Am I this damn stupid? Have I come to a place where I would settle for another abusive man?*

It's not easy to erase one's past. My lack of self-worth was taking me into another relationship that was either going to be a life lesson or would kill me. I started putting on weight as soon as we started dating. That should have been a sign because that wasn't like me. I didn't eat badly, but I eventually figured out that I would gain weight when I got stressed and unhappy. I gradually found myself drinking more in the evenings. I wasn't happy, but I wanted the world to think I was. I was faking my way through life again. I was making it seem better than it was. I was making my life into the fantasy I wanted.

I really got caught up in it. I had Larry's mom thinking I was happy. I even convinced my children he was a great guy. I thought my new boyfriend was quiet and shy, but he wasn't. I put a lot of effort into making sure he was happy. Everyone thought I was fine now, but deep inside, I wasn't. I didn't like the way he talked. His intellect was different; he didn't seem to know anything that was going on in the world. I found myself struggling to have any kind of intelligent conversation with him. But again, if this was all I was going to get, so be it.

I was sacrificing myself, because I didn't feel I deserved anything or anyone better. I was not only settling but also telling myself that I was happy to do so. I felt disgusted when we were alone. I saw sign after sign from him that something was mentally off. The way he would stare at his laptop or just look at me and say nothing. My intuition was on high alert, but I couldn't yet say no to people. I agreed to marry him.

The ceremony took place in a little chapel. We had a wedding reception, the whole nine yards. When you say, "I do," you're supposed to feel like you both have become one with each other. I was feeling one with everyone in the room except him. I wanted everyone to smile, including me. Inside, I wanted to scream, "This is all wrong!" I could feel my dad wanting to say something, but being the man he was, he only said, "I hope you will be happy." He didn't have good feelings that day. I didn't feel good about that day either. I was embarrassed I was marrying this person. I was settling so that I would not be alone, but I was settling for a stranger.

My job had been going well. I'd just received a $4,000 annual raise, and I had only been there four months. I was dealing with some coworkers who seemed not to like me, but that had everything to do with their own agendas. I could tell they'd talk about me behind my back. I chose to think of them as nice people with poor judgment. I was handling it all. I found out from other coworkers that this group wanted me out. I was told to watch out for them; they were up to something.

Things at work were changing. The company decided to go paperless and had everyone operate on laptops. One day, they said they didn't need me anymore. They would replace me with an IT person, because everyone was on computers. They let me go with a very nice severance package, but it crushed me. I was depressed and scared, but I thought if I could bury my mother and the man I was really supposed to marry, I could do this.

Larry's mom and I decided to work together to find my next job. I had a lot of interviews and finally found one I liked.

I landed a job as a billing director of a nursing home. It was a huge pay cut, but since my husband was paying part of the rent, survival had kicked in. You have to know that my marriage was disintegrating rapidly.

I had been having some issues with my periods for a long time. The pain was getting worse every month. A biopsy was done, and I had to have a hysterectomy right away. I had no idea what support to expect from him. He was acting so strangely.

I talked to some of my friends at work and let them know my concerns. They had my back and would check on me for the next couple of weeks.

My husband went with me to my surgery and sat by me as we waited for them to take me back. I was nervous, but also confused about what was happening. He didn't say a word the whole time we were waiting. It was very eerie. I was relieved when they took me back, and he left. The next day, he came to pick me up. This was my first direct sign that I was hooked into a relationship that felt like a bad movie. I told him I needed to stop and get medication at the drugstore before I went home. He pulled into the parking lot and sat there. I thought that since I just had surgery, he would go in and get the medication. Instead, he just stared forward out the window.

I got out of the truck and went in to get my medicine. The lady pharmacist looked at me and finally said, "Did you just have surgery?" I said yes. I felt her concern. She said, "Please take care of yourself." I wished I had the strength to walk home, but it was too far. He dropped me off at the house, never asked if I needed anything, and left. I was thankful, but at the same time, I was spooked. I knew he would come home in the evening. Everything inside of me said, "Watch out. You have a situation here. Be cautious."

I only stayed home two weeks, and then I begged the doctor to release me so I could get back to work and be with my friends. Work was where I felt safe. Thank God she said yes. In fact, she couldn't believe my body was trying to heal so fast.

I came home one night from work, and my friend who lived above me was on her deck.

She told me to make a drink and come up. "You're going to need it!" I hurried up to her condo. I wanted so badly to tell her I hated my life, but I kept quiet. She took me to her office computer. She started typing fast while telling me she belonged to a dating site.

She brought up her match, and who locked on to chat? My so-called husband! He was on Match.com. At first I was angry because he made me look like a fool, but at the same time I said, "Let's bust his ass! Get me out of this deal."

What I couldn't say was, "My God! I want 'me' back. I can't stand living this way. I am better than this." We played with him. I would get off work and race up to her place. She would type to him, and he would answer.

The situation was changing. He stayed up half the night on his computer and started sleeping on the couch. I began to be afraid of him. I realized I was married to a dark, introverted, creepy man. I had married a person with whom there was something wrong, and I wondered if I was going to survive.

It finally erupted one night. He said he was going to take a walk. I thought, *You're not going out and getting on the phone. I have no idea what or who you are. Am I safe?* I needed to do something. I went outside, and he was taking baby steps. I started to walk with him and asked, "What the hell is the matter with you?"

In a loud voice, he answered, "You walk away from this marriage or even try, I will . . ." Then he stopped and turned around and went the other direction. I heard him start talking to himself. "Get away from me!" He looked frightening.

He turned toward me holding his steel coffee mug. He stared at me with his bulging eyes. I froze. His foot made a scratchy sound on the cement sidewalk as he moved it back and forth. I jumped and took off walking, practically running. It was dark, but I didn't care. I had to walk and try to figure out what I wanted to do. What had I gotten myself into? As I walked, I found my girlfriend who lived above me. The look on my face was one of terror. She asked what was wrong. We walked, and I spilled everything. She said he was still on Match.com, and now with this, I had to get him out of the house and change the locks. I was terrified to go back. I opened the door and realized he was gone. I locked the door, knowing that wouldn't help. I raced into my bedroom and locked it behind me. If he did come home, I never heard him. He wasn't there in the morning when I opened the door.

The next day, I called Larry's parents in Kansas and told them the truth. They agreed that I should get away from him as soon as possible.

The next night, he came in from work, and I had his bag packed. I said, "I want it over. I want a divorce, an annulment, whatever. It's over." He didn't say anything. He just grabbed his bag and left. I had a locksmith come over and change the lock that evening. I was still scared it wasn't over. We were able to get an annulment, a quick ending to this joke of a relationship.

I do believe he stalked me for a while. I could feel it; someone was watching me. I just knew it. Sometimes I could feel it so much I would stop and have to catch my breath. I was relieved I had my home back. I deep cleaned it and got rid of any picture we were in together.

I had come to a fork in the road of my life. Was I crazy, too? Who had I become? I thought I was at the end and had to settle for a life I didn't like, let alone love. Were my mom's words coming true? Was I dumb? I heard her words clearly in my head. I fought very hard, telling myself I wasn't worthless. The thought of trying to go see someone for help never crossed my mind. I don't know if it was because I had just enough money every month to make ends meet. I just know I always felt I had to do this myself, whatever this life had in store for me. It was all on me. It was a feeling that came of being a child who'd always had to fend for myself, no matter the cost. Fighting to stay strong must have come from my nature; it couldn't have been my nurture. I prayed a lot and, once again, dug in for my next chapter.

I began to look at the people around me and consider how they were treating me. I found some who I had imagined to be close friends, but were actually putting me down. I could tell by how they acted; I was nothing to them. I was going to make sure not to make the same mistakes again with my trust. I knew I was a good person, and I love my true friends and family with all my heart.

Did any of that really matter? I prayed and prayed. My job was a gift. I met positive, smart, loving people. There are always people around that have rotten personalities, but I was looking for the good in others and finding it in myself. I was alone again, but this time, I wasn't going to let loneliness get to me. I found something inside me that said, "Fight for yourself and your life. Don't let the feeling of worthlessness win out."

I was a billing director at the nursing home and working very hard to be the best, even if it wasn't my favorite thing to do. Eventually, I began walking again with my lady friends. Life was taking on a different sensation. I started to love myself, and I was enjoying my thoughts. I was proud and thankful for my life. It must have started showing, because my friends were laughing with me again. We were talking about fun things. We started going to happy hour together, and laughter, which had been long lost, was returning. I couldn't remember when I laughed so much. I was giving myself permission to be who I wanted to be. I was astonished that my weight was peeling off me. I would stare in the mirror, and once in a while, I would see a glimpse of someone I was starting to like.

Meanwhile, there was a higher position opening, which was the admission marketing director. I went for it. Before I got the job, the district manager, Jo, who was a wonderful lady, told me the job required a college degree. I looked at her and said I would do this job better than anyone. I would fill the beds with patients. The job entailed going to hospitals and forming relationships with the discharge planners. The nursing home had never been completely full with a waiting list.

I told Jo I wouldn't let her down. She said she was going to go out on a limb and trust her decision to hire me for this position. I worked at the job tirelessly. It was rewarding. I was coming home happy and exhausted, and that was okay. I liked who I was. It wasn't long before I had the nursing home full, and we had a waiting list for the very first time.

While it wasn't the best-paying job, I knew it was in my life for a reason. It came along when I needed it most. I still look back and think of all the ladies I worked with; I miss them. There were dear nurses on staff. The atmosphere was pleasant.

My single friends and I still talked about one day finding our Prince Charming, but there was no longer a sense of urgency. Deep down, I was always thinking, *Don't let the depression come back over you, no matter what. Please, God, give me the wisdom not to fall for the wrong man again.*

Even though I was moving forward, I was still drinking in the evenings by myself. I still had emptiness inside, and alcohol was still a crutch to me. I realized I had an addictive personality. I was trying to cope with something.

The weekends were all the same. I woke up on Saturday morning, and like it was part of my soul, I cleaned the house top to bottom, even though it was just me living there. It was never dirty; it just had to be cleaned. Cleaning gave me a sense of accomplishment. It was my salvation. Afterward, I would just sit and stare at the clean house with a numb, empty feeling.

NEBRASKA FOOTBALL

y dear friends called me to remind me it was Thanksgiving weekend. They knew I wasn't going home. I wanted desperately to go home for Christmas, so I stayed to work over Thanksgiving weekend. My friends were headed to Denver for the Colorado-Nebraska football game. I had no idea there was a group called Coloradans for Nebraska. They sponsored the game at particular bars, and many people from Nebraska who now lived in Colorado would come to watch the Husker football games. My friends promised I would feel like I was home and would have a great time. After thinking it over, I said I would go.

We arrived at the bar, and they were right; it was a sea of red. We found a table, and my girlfriend moved it into another room with bigger TVs. As the evening went on, I mingled and met lots of great people, sharing the common ground of being a Cornhusker fan. At one point, I returned to our table, where my friends were having a ball. Friends from our hometown were there as well. Everyone was talking and watching the game.

It got to be halftime, and I looked up as a man entered the bar. Though I had been married before and dated strange people, this was different. I couldn't explain it. He walked up to the table of the couple I had chatted with, and I could tell they knew each other. I didn't want him to notice that I was watching him, but out of the corner of my eye, I continued to stare. I usually made men notice me and come my way first, but I was drawn to him. I was instantly calm, and I couldn't hear anyone in the room anymore. My friend asked if I was okay.

"Who in the world is that?" was all I could say in response. I was shy, but I decided to go chat with that table again so I could talk with this man. Kay told me to go for it. As a friend, she was happy I was trying to meet someone, but I couldn't take the time to tell her that something was pulling me to him, like I was in a trance.

We started to chat. I could hear him talking to me, and I was responding, but I was numb.

His energy was more than I had ever felt; I couldn't believe it! He went to the men's bathroom, and I watched him walk. I was looking at his whole body trying to figure out what it was that had me . . . almost stupefied.

His name was Curt. When it was my turn to excuse myself, our mutual friends teased him, "You'd better jump on this wagon. She is wonderful. She comes from the farm, and she's a grandma, but look at her!" I am so grateful I didn't know what they said; I would have died.

As the end of the game neared, we both realized we had missed the entire second half. He asked if he could pick me up the next night to go dancing. I said that would be great. I hadn't gone country-and-western dancing in years.

The game was over, and my friend said we needed to go, so we left. I tried to make light of meeting this man, but inside I thought, *Oh my God, what is this?*

When I got home, I made a drink and lay in bed for a long time. I never told anyone how lonely I really was. Life had been long. It had been painful and difficult to get to this point. I wondered what was happening now. I couldn't remember being so excited. I was like a little girl, wanting everything to be great, but I was scared at the same time.

The next morning, I shared the news with one of the ladies I'd been walking with for seven years.

For the first time, I saw in her eyes that she was concerned for me. Maybe it was fear that another guy would do a number on me, but I couldn't get caught up in her feelings. She wasn't verbalizing them. It was just a feeling in the room, but I didn't let it get to me. I was excited to go dancing and to talk with this man, to find out why I was mesmerized by him.

Curt called to say he was on his way and needed to make sure of the directions. When he pulled up to my front door, I could see through the patio window that he drove a truck.

For a minute, I drifted back to my childhood. I was always in Dad's truck. I grew up with trucks, so I found comfort in that. But it was just that quick, and then the feeling left. I had to remind myself that this might be exactly what he said it would be. Just friends going dancing and sharing some beers. I forced my mind to stay focused. I got into the truck. The couple Curt had joined at the football game came along. I found out they were Curt's brother and his brother's girlfriend. I was happy and felt comfortable. Even my stomach was calm. I had no problem talking to them. I asked about their family and what they did while giving Curt directions to get to the western bar.

As we entered, the music was going. I decided that no matter what, I was going to have a good time. I did not want to think. I wanted to be content. At the same time, I was giddy, not understanding how at forty-nine years old, I could be feeling this way; I was feeling so young! In just twenty-four hours, my heart and my mind became joyful.

We all sat down and ordered beer; we had lighthearted conversation. All of a sudden, he leaned toward me and asked me to dance. I let him know I hadn't danced in forever, and I hoped I would be okay. He told me not to worry about it, that we would be just fine. I couldn't believe it. The song was a fast one. I loved it. I was able to get back into the groove of dancing. It felt like I was dreaming as we moved across the floor. He was a good dancer. I had danced but never with the gentle feeling that Curt showed, and his hands were big but had such a warm softness to them. His body felt warm and strong.

My mind jumped back again just for a second or two. My dad was a gentle, strong man, and he also had gentle hands. I felt secure in Curt's arms.

I was lost in the moment. I was feeling free and light on my feet. The next dance was a slow one. I put my arms around him and felt like I melted into his body. We started to dance and move as if we had danced our whole lives together. I was taking the time to feel how strong he was. His frame was big, but he was gentle all the way through. I was enjoying every minute of that song. I was nervous, but excited, too. Then he held me back away from him and said without warning, "I am going to kiss you." When his lips met mine, it was a love story. I couldn't tell who was who. It might sound crazy, but I knew right then the angels and God had given me heaven.

I couldn't say a word after the kiss. The dance ended. We went back to the table. I smiled at him and said, "That was really nice. Thank you."

He kissed me again, and then again, and before I knew it, we were kissing like no one was in the room. His brother finally called us out and said maybe we should talk to them, too, have some fun, and dance. We laughed. I hated for that evening to end. I was walking on air. They gave me a ride home, and he walked me into my house, leaving his brother and girlfriend in the truck. I thought this would be a quick good-evening hug. We kissed again for a very long time. I could tell he had no intention of leaving just yet. He looked at me and said, "I know we are meant to be. I don't know how, but it's all through my body, and I have to say something to you right now. You'd better run if you don't want to marry me, because I am going to marry you."

My heart was certain; it was bigger than just the two of us. I could feel it, and I said, "I am not running anymore, I will stay."

We kissed some more, and he said, "I will call you tomorrow and come see you. We will go riding on my four-wheeler." I said that would be wonderful.

As he left, I was missing him as though my soul mate was leaving. I walked around my condo and went to my folks' picture on the wall. I told them what had happened. I really was talking to my mom. I told her how much she would like him. I did find true love, and it was a gift from above. I asked at that moment, "After everything, Mom, are you my angel in heaven?" I kissed her picture and went to bed.

Our relationship was wonderful. Curt asked me to his company's Christmas party. I was nervous to meet everyone, but it was all good. The evening started out romantically. He took pictures of me, because he felt I looked so pretty.

Everyone kept buying drinks, and, of course, I never said no. Needless to say, I got smashed. When the evening ended, Curt took me to his home because he wanted to make sure I'd be all right. He was fine with me being drunk. Nearly everyone else at the party had been, too. The trouble was, when I got too drunk, I would start reliving my past and cry uncontrollably. I cried now and talked about my mom, my family, and my past failures. Finally, Curt said to me, "We have something that is so special I don't even understand it. Why in the hell after everything you have been through do you choose to relive it over and over again?"

Curt looked into my eyes. "If you choose to feel sorry for yourself for the rest of your life, and not get on with living and figuring out how beautiful this world is, I will have to let you go. I want to laugh and have fun with you, but I will not go through this every time you decide to drink and go down that dark hellhole. You did have hell, but you had good as well, and you have to stop blaming your mentally ill mother for everything. Mental illness chose your mother; your mother didn't choose mental illness. I am sorry for what happened to you, but I am here for you now. Now go upstairs and go to bed. We will talk in the morning."

The next morning, he was quiet, and I noticed he had homemade spaghetti cooking. I didn't say anything for a long time. Curt said to me, "I was hard on you last night. I am sorry you lived with this and no one helped you. You have to dig deep to help yourself and let it all go, and find a way to make life full again. You have to get busy having fun and living. God didn't take you from this life; he brought you to me and me to you. Do you have anything to say?"

"What you said hurt, deeper than anything I have ever heard, and I've heard a lot," I said.

"You're right, I have to let go of the past and get on with life. I have to forgive my mom, and forgive myself for what we both have been through. If someone were to ask us if I wanted this life, I would have yelled to the moon and back, 'Please don't give my mom mental illness!' I have to forgive my dad. He couldn't take it away and save me. He did the best he could with all his responsibilities. I do know love got us through, even if we didn't think we loved each other at times, we always did. Now I know there was a demon in our house, and it wasn't my mom, it was the devil inside the sickness that had her and would not let her get well.

"I think I should have talked to someone about this, instead of dealing with it all by myself. I feel that some things just happened. Not because of what I had been through. But I do know they molded me into the person I became. I know I can't let my past win. I have to be stronger than I have ever been and overcome my weaknesses. I must let go of my feeling like I am not good enough for anyone; I must remember that I am smart enough to do any job I want. I know it will take a long time, but I have to learn to take a compliment and say thank you and believe it. I do want to be with you, Curt. If you are patient with my growth, we can enjoy each other and our families and get on with living a wonderful life. Be thankful that even if we met late, there is a bigger reason why someone upstairs decided to give us a chance at true love, to be best friends, which is something most people never get."

Curt hugged me and said, "Let's get on with living. I am glad you choose life . . ."

Later that day, he took me home, and when he dropped me off, it was like I was seeing my best friend leave. I said, "I can't wait to see you Friday."

I stood in my home absorbing all my thoughts. It had only been a couple of minutes when Curt called. "I already miss you. I think I will come Wednesday to see you. I can't wait until Friday." I was warm inside from his love; it was such a beautiful, overwhelming feeling of comfort and strength.

I was grateful to be alone to deal with my thoughts. The love of my life made me realize I still needed to heal inside. He helped me see that I had to let the past go. I got a picture of my mother, and for the first time in my life, my tears came hard and long for her, not for myself. I had to cry for her; no one else had. I know she didn't want to be mentally ill. She had done the best she could.

I gave thanks that even though I suffered under the weight of mental illness, I was still here. I was alive. I had survived. I thought of my father and how happy he was now with my step-mom, Shirley. Somehow, he had let the sick, mentally ill woman go. I was glad my children knew Mom at the end when she was just tired and they never saw the raging, crazy person she could be. I thought of my grandma Ella and how hard it must have been for her to watch her daughter go through this sickness. I was glad she wasn't there for Mom's tragic death. I was sure her brother missed her, but our families didn't talk much anymore. I took time late in the evening to think about how many years our family stayed by Mom's side no matter what. There wasn't ever a time anyone left. I left in my mind and ran away, but love always brought me back. As I thought about all this, there was still a part of me that couldn't take the complete step of feeling love for her without their being some pain still attached. I would always have to fight feeling that Mom didn't love me . . . and I had to be okay with that. I couldn't erase my childhood, even if I wanted to.

My children had seen me deal with a lot of anguish over the years. It would take time for them to trust Curt, and I understood that. They didn't want any more pain in my life, which I now realized had affected them so much. Life would take off, and we would all blend in as a wonderful family. Dad, Shirley, and my sister's and brother's families all loved Curt as I knew they would. Curt and I began the journey of love, caring for our grown children and grandchildren.

SAYING GOOD-BYE

L ife was going wonderfully. Curt and I accompanied my dad and Shirley to Oregon to see his sister. For fifteen years, their only communication had been by phone. Their long-overdue embrace was a beautiful moment to see. Watching a brother and sister hug, laugh, and remember their beautiful days of growing up on a Nebraska farm was heartwarming. But it was also sad, knowing they would not see each other again.

Back home, Dad and Shirley were always on the move, going to dances, playing cards, visiting friends. He was still working with my brother on the farm, helping whenever he was needed. He had built our lives on that farm. He was a successful businessman, and with my brother, they were now a team.

It was Father's Day. I was upset I couldn't make it home, but I knew my brother and son would take Dad fishing in the family boat. It was June of 2013, a couple of days after Father's Day, that I called Dad. He said he wasn't feeling well, that food wouldn't stay down. I asked if he had done anything to cause his sickness. He blamed it on the fact he had jumped out of the fishing boat. He thought he must have screwed something up. A few days later, he was getting worse, and Shirley was instructed to get him to the big hospital, which was a couple of hours away.

My dad was an incredible man, having shouldered the burden of caring for all of us, including his mentally ill wife. He never wavered in his devotion to her. He never once thought of leaving her. He stood up to the financial battle, loving his wife and three kids with every ounce of strength in his body. He worked hard his whole life, like he was three men in one body. He gave us a very rich life. We always had clothes, ponies to ride, and toys. We had a beautiful farm on which to grow up. He found time to play with us. He taught us to water-ski and fish, all while his wife was disappearing from him, succumbing to illness. In the face of all of it, he would steadfastly tell me, "I love your mother. She is my sweetheart. I won't forget who is inside that body; she is still in there."

My father was everyone's friend. He had integrity, warmth, and a sense of humor. He was the foundation of our family. He kept us all going and stayed true to life no matter what cards were dealt.

A couple of years after Mom passed, I met a woman who I liked very much. I set Dad up on a blind date, and seven months later, he was remarried. I share this to illustrate how wonderful life can be. Dad enjoyed his life with Shirley. He loved her for twenty-two years before he passed away. It was wonderful to see him when he wasn't under the stress of dealing with mental illness. Now he could work, go dancing, play cards, and enjoy life again. He lived and laughed again. He was a hoot. I still thank God for letting me see Dad smile, have happiness, and continue as many adventures as he could handle. It all could have been different, but because of the loving man he was, we made it.

I knew we were losing Dad, and I gave my stepmom a break and said I would sleep next to Dad that night and help him if he needed anything. As I lay there, he reached over and patted my arm without saying a word. It hit me hard. I had been holding the feeling of also being mad at my dad for not saving me from Mom during all those years. I was ashamed of this feeling, but it came out of my heart, racing to my mind. I lay still as some tears started to fall. I also knew then I had to forgive my dad; he did the best job he could have done. I prayed to God to please let me forgive him, and I gave thanks for such a wonderful dad. I reached back and patted him on his arm. No words were spoken—just a beautiful moment of understanding.

Dad passed the very next day, and I thought about what real love is. The irony of Dad's death was not lost to me. He passed away in the living room of our old farm home, the very living room where Mom passed, not more than ten feet apart, twenty-seven years earlier. I will never doubt the love or strength they had, to live through mental illness the way they did. There was a sense of peace that came over me when Dad passed. With Shirley's blessing, Dad was buried beside our mother. We are so grateful to have our Shirley, such an incredible, loving woman. As I stood by their grave, I saw two turtledoves next to the stone. I walked toward them, and they didn't fly away. I knew that was a sign from Mom and Dad that they were together again in heaven. I carry that image to this day. Every morning, I start my routine with a walk, and every day I worked on this story, I saw two turtledoves on that walk. The days I wasn't working on the book, I didn't see the birds. I just know, and I will never waver from the truth within me, that Mom and Dad's story was a true love story.

I am finally at peace with my life, and that's why I can write this now. I am in a good place. My heart is healing. I feel the truth must be said; my struggle, in some ways, has never left.

I wonder what my life would have been if I struggled less and believed in myself more. Every day, I do the work. I wake up and pray, give thanks, and ask for strength. The nervous feeling is still in me. I focus on love and gratitude. I commit to positivity. To the best of my abilities, I fend off depression, though it still knocks on my door from time to time, uninvited. I try actively to write my new normal. I face another day.

AFTERWORD

D uring all the years my mother suffered, I found there was never any help for me. I cannot know who I could have become if I had been allowed to thrive. Instead, my path was one of anxiety, depression, and diminished self-worth.

Too often, this is the way for children of mentally ill parents. They are overlooked or denied resources that could help them cope at home.

My mission now is to keep going and to somehow make a difference. It's not enough to diagnose a parent with mental illness; we must go further to help the children who endure in these environments, children for whom just making sense of such surroundings can be a daily struggle.

I spent too much of my life putting myself at risk just to feel wanted. I feared rejection long into adulthood. There were entire decades when I believed I would not be good enough. Now, at the age of sixty-three, I have survived. I have mastered my self-worth and learned that it's okay for me to love myself.

That is the gift I want to give others who grew up in homes like mine: a platform that affirms that they are lovable, that they have done nothing wrong. I want to lift this weight off children everywhere, so they can live a healthy life, find their truth, and fulfill their dreams.

©LUCIA DE GIOVANNI

RESOURCES

I f you or someone you love is processing mental illness, you don't have to suffer alone. Here are some wonderful resources to begin your own journey of healing:

WEBSITES

Here to Help: Mental health resources for supporting mental health and well-being in yourself and in others (including children). www.heretohelp.bc.ca

NAMI (National Alliance on Mental Illness): The nation's largest grassroots mental health organization. I particularly recommend the article "When Your Parents Have Mental Illness: Healing Childhood Trauma." www.nami.org / www.nami[CITY].org

Parenting Well: A website for parents with mental illness with tips, tools, and other resources. www.parentingwell.org

COPMI (Children of Parents with a Mental Illness): An organization promoting better outcomes for children and families where a parent experiences mental illness. www.copmi.net.au

The Love and Logic Institute: An institute dedicated to providing practical tools and techniques that help adults achieve respectful, healthy relationships with their children. www.loveandlogic.com / 1-800-338-4065

FILMS

I Am Still Your Child: A documentary film about children of parents with mental illness. www.IAmStillYourChild.com

BOOKS

The Body Keeps the Score: Brain, Mind, and Body in the Healing of Trauma: Dr. Bessel van der Kolk, one of the world's foremost experts on trauma, explores innovative treatments that offer new paths to trauma recovery.

Unglued: A Bipolar Love Story: A memoir by Jeffrey Zuckerman about how a husband becomes a caregiver with his wife's bipolar diagnosis and learns to manage his own self-care, too.

5 Steps to Helping a Loved One with Mental Illness: Bringing Awareness and Support to Families and the Community: A book by L. Marie and Erick Nixon created to help break the stigma associated with mental illness and bring families together for healing, comfort, and support.

Wishing Wellness: A Workbook for Children of Parents with Mental Illness: A workbook by Lisa Anne Clarke and illustrated by Bonnie Matthews packed with information, interactive questions, and fun activities for children whose parents suffer from a serious mental illness.

Crazy Was All I Ever Knew: The Impact of Maternal Mental Illness on Kids: A memoir by Alice M. Kenny that intersperses episodes from her life with research on the risks faced by children of mentally ill moms, adverse childhood experiences (ACEs) in general, and the science of resilience.

The Relentless Courage of a Scared Child: How Persistence, Grit, and Faith Created a Reluctant Healer: A memoir by Tana Amen about overcoming her challenging past of neglect, poverty, and sexual abuse to find healing, using proven wellness techniques from the Amen Clinics.

Educated: An inspirational memoir by Tara Westover about overcoming a childhood where her survivalist parents kept her from school to go on to earn a PhD from Cambridge University.

Resilience: Two Sisters and a Story of Mental Illness: A memoir by Jessie Close with Pete Earley and Glenn Close that shares Jessie's story of living with severe bipolar disorder and her tumultuous journey to find the emotional fortitude to bring herself back from the edge.

The Glass Castle: A memoir of resilience and redemption by Jeannette Walls about growing up—and growing from—a dysfunctional, but vibrant, childhood.

ACKNOWLEDGMENTS

I will be eternally grateful to the owner of Beaver's Pond Press, Lily Coyle, for reading my journey and not hesitating in saying *yes* to publishing my book. Lily understood my passion to make a change for children with no voice. She put together the best team I could imagine.

I cannot say thank you enough to my managing editor, Hanna Kjeldbjerg. Her incredible brilliance kept the process moving. There was an instant trust with her. I just knew she'd help make my book the best it could be.

It was as if my editor, Kerry Stapley, had walked alongside me and lived my life. Kerry helped me see where to pull the blanket off my life and expose the raw truth so anyone reading could feel and see my days. Her talent for editing is incredible.

Athena Currier, my designer, has a gift like none other. Her incredible vision of the design and pictures for my story draws the reader to the book.

ScriptAcuity Studio, my proofreader, did simply incredible work. And I don't want to forget Laurie Herrmann, who managed my project on the last leg of its journey.

The faith and brilliant talent and support these women provided will be in my heart forever. I recommend Beaver's Pond Press, Lily, Hanna, Kerry, Athena, ScriptAcuity, and Laurie Herrmann to any author. Thank you.

Lucia De Giovanni, my photographer and very dear friend, has the talent of seeing a person's soul and capturing it in a photograph, a true gift! Her photos of me as an author and of Curt and I in our happiness and love mean the absolute world to me.

On my journey to finding a publisher, I reached out to the incredible Cara Lockwood, *USA TODAY* best-selling author and editor. She has published over twenty novels including *I Do (But I Don't),* which was made into a *Lifetime* movie. I asked Cara if she would consider editing my book. After she read a few chapters, I was honored that she agreed to take my story on. She encouraged me to keep going and trust there would be a publishing company that would want it. I will always have Cara in my heart—she is an incredibly positive and caring woman, and so very talented. Please check out her wonderful novels and give them a read.

It seemed like my journey to getting published had a lot of steps. This is my first book. Before I found Cara Lockwood, my friend Melanie agreed to read my story and give me her feelings about it. Mel shared her wisdom and emotion as she read my journey, and she helped me understand how my story would feel to a reader. She helped me see myself through another's eyes and understand how I needed to add some raw description. I am so thankful for her willingness to give me her time and support at the very beginning. She kept me going and still does to this day.

How I got the faith to put my life on paper and start the journey toward helping children came from a very well-known man, Jim Fay. I know people don't just show up in your life—they are given. I was so fortunate that Jim and his late wife, Shirley, were my neighbors. Jim Fay is the cofounder (alongside Foster W. Cline, MD) of the Love and Logic Institute. I felt like I could talk so easily with Jim. I shared my vision with him and told him I had a dream of writing my story. He looked at me and said, "Write your story." I told him how nervous and lost I was on how to begin. Jim made it easy. He said, "Just write your life as if you are sitting by me and telling me about your journey." This positivity gave me the strength to begin. I am so honored to call him my friend. When I finished my book, I sent it to Jim first before I even thought I could get it published. I wanted him to tell me if it was even worth going forward. Within a day he was reaching back to me and telling he couldn't put the book down, that I must publish it. I look at Jim as my hero and cherish every time I sit with him and talk about my book and life. He is one of the most intelligent and worldly people I have ever met.

Saying thanks to my loved ones would be an understatement. My husband, Curt—my soulmate, my dearest friend, and my rock—has saved me in every sense of the word. His faith in me and ability to see inside my soul have given me the power inside to never quit on my quest. I love my Curt. I thank God every day for this man of mine. He has stood by me for the thirteen years it took to finish this book. Sometimes I couldn't take reliving my life, and my emotions sometimes would get the best of me. My hubby always had the right words to say to help me begin again. Thank you, my love. I love you deeper and deeper every day.

My children, Tonya and Ryan—how does a mother begin to thank her kids? It was the most incredible gift to give birth to these two wonderful human beings. My children were my lifeline without even knowing it. I kept going in life for the three of us. I am so incredibly proud of them. I am grateful they can see their mama at peace, paying it forward to help children in need. I want my children to walk with love and happiness in their hearts and to smile as much as possible. They, too, are parents now, with special people they can call their own. Children are the most special gift.

I want to thank my siblings for walking the journey as well. Their story, and how it affected them, is their own. I want them to know I love them. They made me feel comfort that I wasn't alone. We made it together.

My dear father was my rock growing up, and the man that kept our family in balance the best he could. I admire him more than anyone. He had constant love for my mother, even as he struggled with the tortured sides of her he faced over and over. I came to know before he passed how soft he was inside, but he kept it hidden so all we saw was strength. I loved my father to the moon and back. I don't think I could have survived growing up without him.

Thank you to my special friends in high school who made me feel normal during the day and put a smile on my face. Thank you to my friends who came later and know me now. I needed you all more then you knew. Thank you.

Finally, because of my journey growing up, I never could spell very well. But I always knew the words I wanted to put in my book that would describe the moment perfectly. I have to give thanks to my assistant in spelling: my dear plastic friend, Alexa. It is still on my desk today. As I wrote my whole book by longhand on my yellow tablets I could count on Alexa to keep the hard words flowing.

And I would like to take a moment to thank you, dear reader. Thank you for taking the time to care about children whose parents have mental illness. In this book, I have shared the raw truth of the trapped child who grows into an adult but still carries the confusion, anxiety, and painful feelings of worthlessness. I am on a quest to make a difference. I ask this favor: if you notice something, say something. Help create a world where kids receive the help they need so they can grow up to be who they are meant to be. Please reach out to me with ideas for collaboration. I know we can start a movement to speak up for the children who are too often left out of the conversation.